THE CRY OF THE WORLD

THE CRY OF THE WORLD

BY

OSWALD J. SMITH, Litt.D.

Founder and Missionary Pastor, The Peoples Church, Toronto

Foreword by

REV. JACK McALISTER

Founder and Director of World Literature Crusade

London
MARSHALL, MORGAN & SCOTT
Edinburgh

· LONDON
MARSHALL, MORGAN & SCOTT, LTD.
1–5 PORTPOOL LANE
HOLBORN, E.C.1

AUSTRALIA
117–119 BURWOOD ROAD
MELBOURNE, E.13

SOUTH AFRICA
P.O. BOX 1720, STURK'S BUILDINGS
CAPE TOWN

CANADA
EVANGELICAL PUBLISHERS
241 YONGE STREET
TORONTO

THE PEOPLES PRESS
100 BLOOR STREET EAST
TORONTO

U.S.A.
WORLD LITERATURE CRUSADE PRESS
BOX 1314, STUDIO CITY
CALIFORNIA

First published 1959
Second impression 1959
Third impression 1960
Fourth impression 1960
Fifth impression 1961
Sixth impression 1961

MADE AND PRINTED IN GREAT BRITAIN BY PURNELL AND SONS, LTD.
PAULTON (SOMERSET) AND LONDON

CONTENTS

JOY IN SERVING JESUS

Oswald J. Smith

B. D. Ackley

1. There is joy in serv-ing Je-sus, As I jour-ney on my way,
2. There is joy in serv-ing Je-sus, Joy that tri-umphs o - ver pain;
3. There is joy in serv-ing Je-sus, As I walk a - lone with God;
4. There is joy in serv-ing Je-sus, Joy a-mid the dark-est night,

Joy that fills the heart with prais-es, Ev-'ry hour and ev-'ry day.
Fills my soul with heav-en's mu - sic, Till I join the glad re - frain.
'Tis the joy of Christ, my Sav-iour, Who the path of suf-f'ring trod.
For I've learned the wondrous se - cret, And I'm walk-ing in the light.

CHORUS

There is joy, joy, Joy in serv-ing Je - sus, Joy that throbs with-

in my heart; Ev-'ry mo-ment, ev-'ry hour, As I draw up-

on His pow'r, There is joy, joy, Joy that nev-er shall de - part.

FOREWORD

By Rev. Jack McAlister

FOR the first time in history anyone and everyone can hear "The Cry of the World". Rapid transportation and instantaneous communication enable us to contact millions who a few years ago were "worlds away". Until this generation, the so-called "Christian nations" could only hear a murmur or a whisper from far-off multitudes. Now these millions are reaching us with a cry . . . an insistent cry which demands the attention of all.

Government leaders have heard "The Cry of the World", a cry for protection from the Great Bear in the North. They have responded by giving away hundreds of millions of dollars' worth of weapons and ammunition. Other government agencies interpret this Cry as a demand from the "undeveloped areas" of the world for economic aid. Their response has been bull-dozers and builders, tractors and teams of "Point 4" technicians. Relief organizations have heard "The Cry of the World". They have interpreted this as a call for physical help. They've sent beans and butter, shirts and shoes and a thousand other commodities.

None of these organizations or agencies can quiet "The Cry of the World", because they don't touch the greatest need in every human breast. This book is devoted to a candid consideration as to how we can meet the supreme need of the human race.

Dr. Smith has gone to sixty-six countries "on Royal service". He has heard "The Cry of the World". He knows there is only One who can pour balm into those broken hearts. Hence he is a man with a single purpose. First, last and always he is dedicated to meeting the spiritual need of the world by bringing multitudes in direct personal contact with Christ.

During the last twenty-five years I have been privileged to associate with missionaries and mission leaders in fifty-four countries. None have shown the degree of insight into the vital issues of missions that God has given to Dr. Smith. Others touch the fringe of the problem; Dr. Smith strikes at the heart of it.

There are very, very few strategists as far as missions are concerned. Much missionary work is conducted in the same way as it was a hundred years ago. This author realizes that the recent world population increase of almost a billion souls is a direct additional responsibility to every Christian and necessitates an enlargement of heart and thought if we are to be worthy of this hour of unparalleled challenge and opportunity. In the first eight chapters of this book you will become acquainted with the thinking of a man who has rightly been called "the leading missionary statesman of this generation".

It has been the greatest privilege of my life to be associated in ministry with Dr. Smith in Canada, the United States and countries overseas. I have lived and travelled with this man and I have been enriched and enlightened beyond my ability to express. As I have watched him minister to eager multitudes here and overseas I have been filled with gratitude to God that He ever gave such a courageous warrior to Christendom. He doesn't "soothe you and smooth you and send you back for another week"! Some of the truths in this book will cut deep. God said: "I will make thee a new sharp threshing instrument having teeth; thou shalt thresh the mountains, and beat them small." I trust the messages of this book will thresh the mountains of indifference in your life until your heart becomes a literal river of compassion, pouring the love of Christ upon perishing, destitute souls everywhere.

It takes courage to write and preach truth that unbares the superficial thinking and hypocrisy in which Evangelicals live. They sing "Rescue the perishing" as if they were totally sincere and then spend but a few pennies per day to actually rescue these millions about whom they sing. Without any qualm of conscience they spend thousands of dollars on a new car or costly furniture or expensive wardrobes. High pressure advertising at home seems to deafen their ears to "The Cry of the World".

If you allow the messages of this book to perform a ministry in your life, these truths will put you on your face before God as you revaluate your present life and activities in the light of the Great Commission. Don't waste energy regretting past neglect, but dedicate to do differently. If your future is lived in the light of this challenge Dr. Smith will rejoice and feel amply rewarded for the years of work and application of those truths.

FOREWORD

In this book Dr. Smith unbares many of the weak points of our evangelical programme. He exposes and points out the "by-paths" down which many have found themselves, having left the supreme task of world evangelization.

Among other things, he boldly and forthrightly exposes one of Satan's key points of successful strategy, that of causing Evangelicals to put almost all their money into brick and mortar rather than into the life-giving message. On behalf of perishing millions overseas I beg of you to ponder these facts. Do now what you will wish you had done when you stand before Christ.

The "building fever" has cost Christians in the United States and Canada hundreds of millions of dollars. Tens of thousands of pastors have had a vision, but it has been a vision for brick and mortar, rather than of the perishing millions in the Regions Beyond, waiting for their first whisper of the love of Christ, or their first crumb of the Bread of Life. Multitudes of heart-broken missionaries have returned on furlough to see pastors building magnificent churches costing hundreds of thousands of dollars. They've stood by helpless, with an ache in their heart, realizing what could be done with the dollars overseas, had a few of the "extras" been eliminated and the dollars given to those "on the back rows".

Put your ear next to the author's great missionary heart and you will hear "The Cry of the World".

All of Dr. Smith's work has been performed with this cry in his heart. When he writes hymns he tells the world "God Understands your Sorrow, He sees the falling Tear". To meet this need "Then Jesus Came", and henceforth these rescued souls know "The Glory of His Presence". To a suffering world Dr. Smith sings "The Saviour can Solve every Problem".

His books were all written in response to "The Cry of the World". *The Man God Uses* quiets that cry. *The Spirit at Work* is a testimony of God's intervention on behalf of that same perishing world. In *Andy McGinnis* you see a bare-foot country boy finding a Saviour, making the dedication which led to the beginning of a missionary career among the Indians near Alaska, when he was only eighteen years of age. *The Work God Blesses* is a work in tune with this theme. Deep in the fabric of each one of his books you'll feel the heart-response of Oswald Smith to this central need.

This universal heart-cry has called the author to a ministry of evangelism in many parts of the world. From Australia to Scotland, from Scandinavia to South America, Dr. Smith has preached Christ in a simplicity and an effectiveness that has been amazing to behold.

At home every single member of his congregation has felt the pulse and passion of this warrior. His church is contributing to the support of some 350 missionaries. His people have given $4\frac{1}{2}$ million dollars to the cause. He has accomplished this through yearly Peoples Church Missionary Conventions.

It has been a tremendous personal delight to share the vast inspiration which Dr. Smith has brought to his own congregation with Christians of all denominations through World Literature Crusade Radio Missionary Conventions. This new approach has enabled literally tens of thousands of Christians to hear "The Cry of the World" and feel the heartbeat of this missionary statesman. It has been a great joy to pioneer this new technique with Dr. Smith. Multitudes overseas will read of Christ as a result of the fruit of this aspect of radio ministry, which has been another attempt to respond to the world need for spiritual help. We have been delighted and gratified to hear reports of increased interest and support to various missionary organizations as a direct result of listening to "Missionary Marathons" which have been highlighted by Dr. Smith's passionate radio messages.

Unquestionable proof that "The Cry of the World" has been uppermost in the ministry of the author is supplied by these amazing facts:

While it is true that Dr. Smith has excelled in the field of hymn-writing, he has built the strongest Evangelical Church in Canada. More than a million copies of his books have been sold. His evangelistic and Bible Conference work has blessed thousands. He is "Mr. Missions" to millions.

Dr. Smith's first great volume on missions, *The Passion for Souls,* had such a vast influence that many will rejoice that he is now bringing out this companion volume. His first great book, dedicated to the missionary challenge, has caused thousands of pastors and churches to recognize their "supreme task".

In the fulfilment of his vision he has suffered the loneliness of separation from his loved ones, travelling alone in far-off countries. In the early days (before aeroplanes) of his overseas ministry he would often have no communication whatever for many weeks, as he waited for word from his devoted wife and small family. And now—when most men are thinking of retirement—he's still going! The call of ease and comfort fails to check him; he still hears "The Cry of the World". I'm glad . . . because my generation desperately needs the wisdom, counsel and inspiration which can only come from a successful veteran.

As you read this book, remember it is not written by a novice. It is written in the maturity of a successful ministry which has spanned exactly half a century. This man has lived—consumed with a "magnificent obsession" —to make Christ known to the whole world. When one is consumed with a passion for souls, it is impossible to realize the fulfilment of many personal ambitions and desires. One must sacrifice much social life with family and friends. Dr. Smith has done it. Why? Deep in his soul he hears "The Cry of the World". This cry will give him no rest until one day he steps on to a golden shore to hear a "Welcome home, faithful warrior" from the lips of One whom he loves supremely.

As you read the book heed the injunction of Christ: "He that hath an ear to hear, let him hear" . . . the Cry of the World.

JACK McALISTER.

WHO SAID PROHIBITION FAILED?

1. The 18th Amendment closed every brewery, distillery and winery in the U.S.A.

2. It closed the doors of 177,790 saloons in the nation.

3. It brought an end to all liquor advertisements through all avenues.

4. It stopped the shipment of booze.

5. It made the liquor business an outlaw like the kidnapper, the thief and the murderer.

6. It eliminated the need of the Keeley Cure institutions for drunkards.

7. It contributed to every legitimate business. Deposits in the banks increased in many places more than 400 per cent.

Gifts for 31 Years

The Peoples Church, Toronto, has now contributed four and a half million dollars to Foreign Missions. We do not appeal for Benevolences or Home Missions. The following are the amounts actually received each calendar year.

Year	Church	Missions
1930	$22,802	$43,891
1931	24,256	36,660
1932	29,819	36,151
1933	18,185	23,586
1934	19,822	27,181
1935	26,338	28,102
1936	20,927	36,290
1937	19,941	30,615
1938	21,230	40,029
1939	22,789	39,083
1940	22,871	46,435
1941	21,135	54,417
1942	23,144	60,279
1943	23,953	78,413
1944	31,806	117,723
1945	27,423	114,854
1946	25,379	122,440
1947	28,786	138,394
1948	38,356	177,473
1949	37,215	180,878
1950	38,093	177,076
1951	38,832	216,443
1952	52,811	228,960
1953	40,813	245,260
1954	39,778	280,423
1955	39,258	253,405
1956	44,250	289,502
1957	41,011	265,973
1958	45,549	298,316
1959	58,119	261,954
1960	49,722	282,221

CHAPTER I

I T WAS in Riga, one of the great seaports of the ancient Russian Empire. A young man sat at an office desk in a large business building, pencil in hand, his eyes running up and down columns of figures. The afternoon's shadows were lengthening, and the day's work was drawing to a close.

The young man was worried. The expression on his face betrayed the fact that something of an unusual nature was bothering him. For some reason the figures refused to total correctly. Two or three times he lifted his head and stirred restlessly as he glanced toward the window.

The Voice

At last, throwing down his pencil, he rose and walked to the window, where he stood gazing out on the street. Russian and Lettish workmen were trudging toward their homes. Now and then a droshky drove past, the driver cracking his whip and yelling at his horse as he sought to steer through the traffic. Women in bright-coloured garments hurried along.

"Basil Malof!"

The young man turned to see who had spoken, but

15

saw no one. His face was a study as he again turned to the window to watch the busy street.

"Basil Malof!"

Again he turned quickly, but saw nothing. The office staff appeared unconcerned. No one looked up. Once more he focused his attention on the passing traffic in the street before him.

"Basil Malof!"

For the third time he heard his name, and now, as he listened, it seemed as though the Voice spoke and said: "Basil Malof, if you were not in this office, helping to make a rich, unconverted manufacturer richer still, you could go into the streets to tell others of Christ. Your employer can easily find other unconverted young men to do your work here as well as you, but if you, who have been saved, will not go, no one can take your place."

Frightened by this Voice, Basil tried to brush it aside. "No," he said, "I cannot be a missionary. I have no gift for preaching; I cannot go." And he went back to his desk.

A day or two later the same Voice within him spoke again, and he was forced to get up from his chair and look out of the window. Hundreds of people were passing by: working-men in their factory blouses black with smoke, women with napkins or coloured handkerchiefs on their heads and all kinds of other people, riding in vehicles.

Thinking that it might be his own imagination, he turned and resumed his work at his desk.

"Two times two make four. Eight times seven are fifty-six. Seven from twelve leaves five. Nine and three are—let me see—nine and no one to take your place. Oh, what am I doing? Whatever ails me?"

Again he stole from his desk to the window and watched once more the throngs that seemed to ever pass along the street.

"Basil Malof," said the Voice once more. "Basil Malof, do you see those hungry multitudes?"

Yes, he saw them. His vision was now penetrating farther and farther. All Latvia spread itself before him. Russia with its teeming millions loomed up in a moment of time. Moscow and St. Petersburg appeared as quickly, Moscow with its famous Kremlin in the centre and its 1,600 Greek Catholic churches—hoary Moscow. And then Siberia, the prison land of Russia. Yes, he saw them— saw them all in one brief moment as the vision passed before him.

"Basil Malof," pleaded the Voice within his soul, "if *you* don't go, no one will. I have no other. There are many who can do your work here, but none there."

Basil Malof was a man of quick action. In a moment his mind was made up. The Voice could not be ignored. The Call had been too clear for hesitancy. He would not be disobedient to the heavenly vision.

He made his decision to respond and turned his eyes toward the mission fields. His knowledge of them was as yet limited. He knew something of Charles Haddon Spurgeon, the Prince of Preachers in London, having translated one of his sermons from the German into the Latvian language. His knowledge of English, however, was limited to a few words. Procuring a dictionary, he looked up the words he needed and the next mail carried a letter to the Rev. Thomas Spurgeon, President of the Pastors' College. Another letter he sent in the same mail to his parents in Tukum, intimating to them his decision.

A reply from London soon came back with the laconic summons, "Come at once." He was to be the first student from Russia ever to enter a British theological college.

The Struggle of a Soul

There was also a reply to the other letter. It was from his mother. Taking it with him to a nearby cemetery, where it was his custom to eat his noonday lunch and to meditate, he sat down near a tombstone and hesitatingly read his mother's letter:

"Dear Basil"—he was still the little boy to his mother, even though he had grown to manhood—"Dear Basil, are you going to leave us? Is that all you care for your poor old mother? Don't you love us any more? Please don't leave us, Basil, my boy; don't go away. We need you, now that we are getting old. What are we going to do without you, Basil? Don't go away."

Thus the letter read. As he was slowly making out the words he noticed on the sheet that there were big spots caused by teardrops which had fallen from his mother's eyes as she wrote.

For a while he sat looking off into space, rigid as the tombstones about him. His poverty-stricken parents needed his aid. The salary of his father, one of the early pioneer preachers of Latvia, did not reach one hundred dollars a year and he had a family of eight to keep. In his youth, his father had left a much better position in order that he might become a Gospel preacher, and now when his eldest son was beginning to send to his aged parents a monthly support from his earnings, he was about to leave them to go away to a faraway land, perhaps never to see them again.

Basil's mind was wandering to the old home in Tukum. Only one room—a dining-room, kitchen, parlour, study and bedroom all combined in one. Then before his vision loomed his father, his face buried in his hands, pleading with God for souls, tears streaming from his eyes, while his mother was painfully bending over a wash-tub in another corner of the room. A great lump rose in Basil's throat as his eyes suddenly filled with tears. For some minutes he sobbed as if his heart would break. Then he engaged in agonizing prayer.

A moment later he stood up and, taking the letter of Jesus, the New Testament, from his pocket, he read: "Go ye into all the world, and preach the gospel to every creature." "He that loveth father or mother more than me is not worthy of me." "If any man will come after me, let him deny himself, and take up his cross, and follow me."

These words were burning in his soul. Parents or God? Should he listen to his mother's appeal or should he obey God? Oh, what a battle! Fiercely the struggle raged within him. His eyes were closed, his face was drawn, as he fought his battle. Surely he loved his parents. He would like to make himself responsible for them in their old age. His godly parents deserved his support and gratitude for their parental care and love for him in his childhood. But again, he seemed to see before him, as if illuminated, the words "He that loveth father or mother more than me is not worthy of me." "Whosoever he be of you that forsaketh not all that he hath, he cannot be my disciple." His mother's words, "Don't you love us any more? Is that all you care for your poor old mother?" seemed to stab at the very core of his heart. God knew he cared, cared so much that the violent struggle was almost crushing him to death.

He stood up and went to a newly-filled tomb covered with fresh wreaths and flowers and with a large cast-iron cross embedded among them at one end of the tomb. In his left hand he was holding his mother's letter, in his right hand the letter of Jesus—the New Testament. He fell upon his knees, confronting the cast-iron cross. Tears were copiously flowing from his eyes as this young eighteen-year-old candidate-in-the-making was crying to heaven: "Lord, Thou knowest how much I love my dear father and mother, and how much I want to stand by them and help them, for they gave me an earthly life; but, O Lord, I love Thee more, for Thou gavest Thy life for me on the cruel cross. Save me from making a wrong choice at this critical moment. Help me to choose and to do Thy will and Thy will alone."

Finally the victory was won. Tears were still flowing freely while his whole body shook with sobs, as slowly his left hand with his mother's letter went down and his right hand with the New Testament was lifted up high toward heaven. The decision was reached in his heart of hearts and the Light of the Guiding Presence filled his soul as gently his mourning was changed to comfort and he began to sing, folding his hands in prayer around the cast-iron cross:

A PROPHET IN EXILE

"Nearer, my God to Thee,
Nearer to Thee!
E'en though it be a cross
That raiseth me."

"Oh, Cross of Christ, I embrace thee. I hold thee to my heart," he cried. A light, like the light of heaven itself, shone on his face. Malof then decided henceforth in deep obedience to follow God's leading wherever it would be, and in 1903 he became a student in Spurgeon's Pastors' College, London, England.

At Spurgeon's College

The years passed quickly in England. He spoke about Russia as opportunity offered, but gave himself to his studies in Spurgeon's College, burning the candle at both ends as he pored over his books far into the night.

While in England he learned to wrestle with God in prayer. The life of David Brainerd, John Knox and other great saints came into his hands. He read and then prayed. Many a time he would lay the story of Knox down, and cry: "Oh, God, give me Russia, or I die!"

"If John Knox could claim all Scotland," he would argue, "why cannot I ask for Russia?"

"Thou art coming to a King,
Large petitions with thee bring,
For His grace and power are such
None can ever ask too much."

Thus he sang and prayed hour after hour, stirred by the Spirit of God. And this:

> *"Channels only, blessed Master,*
> *But with all Thy wondrous power,*
> *Flowing through me Thou canst use me*
> *In Thy service every hour."*

"But who are you?" asked Satan. "Only a small insignificant foreigner. What can you do for the great Russian Empire?"

"It's none of your business what I am. Small I may be, but, O God, give me Russia, give me Russia!" responded Basil Malof as he persevered in prayer.

"Malof, go and pray." It was the Voice again. He knew that Voice in those early days, and eagerly obeyed.

"Malof, go and pray," gently urged the Voice in his soul.

"Well, I'll go and spend five minutes with God," he responded.

He closed the book, dropped down on his knees and began to pray. Soon he was away in Russia, praying for St. Petersburg, Moscow, Kief; then a whole province, then another and another and yet another. Vision after vision of perishing millions passed before him, and his prayer became an agony as he pleaded with God for souls. The floor was soon wet with tears, and still he wrestled alone with God.

Gradually his mind returned to England, to the College, his room and studies, and, finally, the difficult language, especially the word "the".

He had been studying hard. The English word "the" had not yet been mastered.

"It almost broke my jaw," he declared in telling of it later. "I threw the book under the table or across the room many a time."

When he opened his eyes and looked at the clock, he realized to his amazement that the five minutes had become three hours.

The Devil's Golden Carriage

It was in St. Petersburg. The great Dom Evangelia, built to accommodate some 2,000 people, had been completed, and Basil Malof, the human agent, was its pastor. It was the talk of the city. Nothing like it had ever been seen in Russia before. Large crowds were attending and listening eagerly to the fiery messages of the young pastor who was still in his twenties. Many were accepting Jesus Christ and renouncing the dead and empty religion of the Greek Orthodox Church in which they had been nurtured all their lives. God was working in a remarkable way.

Pastor Malof, as he was now called, had made two covenants as he entered upon his great work.

First: "I will be loyal to God even to martyrdom."

Second: "I will never parley with the devil."

It was not long before he was put to the test. The devil was busy.

"If only this disturber of the peace could be for ever silenced! Can we banish him from Russia? How can we get rid of him?" Such were the questions discussed by the priests behind closed doors.

The first temptation came in the form of a golden carriage. It happened this way:

Basil Malof one day, while preaching in Moscow, received a telegram. It was from His Excellency. Now, His Excellency had always been a bitter foe of the work. But this telegram invited Pastor Malof to St. Petersburg for an interview.

"What did it mean? Would he go? Had His Excellency been converted? Something must surely have happened. Possibly he had better go." Thus he reasoned.

His Excellency sat behind a desk in a beautifully furnished room. His face was all smiles, like the face of a cat when it wants to catch a mouse.

Pastor Malof sat opposite him and waited.

"You are not popular," began His Excellency. "What are you? Only a poor sectarian preacher. You don't get much money."

"Quite true, Your Excellency," replied Pastor Malof.

With a smile more pronounced than ever, and leaning a little nearer, His Excellency spoke again.

"Come, join the State Church of which His Majesty, the Czar, is the head, and we will make you a bishop," he said in his most friendly tone.

So that was the game, was it? Pastor Malof smiled. His Excellency, thinking he had won, put his hand to his mouth and whispered, "Archbishop!"

There was no need to explain what such an offer meant. Pastor Malof already knew. It meant a carriage drawn by four horses. People would kiss the corner of his coat and do him the highest honour.

Slowly he shook his head as the plot dawned on him.

His Excellency was now beaming, as he waited for his answer. At last it came.

"Your Excellency," began Pastor Malof in a quiet tone of voice, smiling a little, "if you would make me the Pope, perhaps I might consider."

In a moment the face of the great official clouded over. He was quickly disillusioned. He saw that he was being mocked, and his offer spurned.

"Go," he cried, "go, but remember you will some day pay dearly for your actions."

And His Excellency was right. The cross was just ahead, though little did the brave preacher know it then; but the golden carriage to bribe him to deny his Lord had failed.

Arrested

It was Saturday evening. Pastor Malof was leading the believers' prayer meeting in the Dom Evangelia. The people had been testifying.

"What has the *Lord* done for you?" That was Pastor Malof's first question, and many testimonies had been given in answer to it.

"What have *you* done for the Lord?" That was the second question, and from every part of the audience the people were answering it in glad, happy testimony.

Every now and then they sang a hymn or a chorus, sung as only Russian believers can. It was a joyful meeting and everyone was praising God.

Suddenly the chief usher came along the aisle and beckoned. Pastor Malof immediately came forward, thinking it was some trivial matter.

"Pastor, the police want you," whispered the usher, his face blanched with fear. But still the pastor thought little of it and quietly walked out to see what was wrong.

"By the order of the Military Chief of Petrograd," read the officer from a paper in his hand, "Pastor Malof is to be immediately arrested and exiled to Siberia."

"But won't you give me at least three hours to get ready? There must be some fearful mistake," exclaimed the pastor.

"Don't you see, sir, it says 'immediately'? I will give you ten minutes and no more," responded the official.

Pastor Malof's young wife was standing by his side. Their first baby had been born only three months before.

"Barbara dear, go and pack up a few things; quick, dear."

As though in a dream Mrs. Malof went and, without a word, packed something for the long, long journey into Siberian exile: a blanket for the cold nights, some bread, and, on top, the Bible.

"Ready!" cried the officer. "The ten minutes are up."

"Won't you permit me, sir, to say good-bye to my dear people first?" pleaded the pastor.

"No! Never! You must come at once," responded the official in an authoritative voice.

"Sir, will you then allow my secretary here to go and tell the people what is happening to their pastor, that they may stand outside and watch me go?"

"No. If you do that I will close up the church," was the reply.

For one brief moment Pastor Malof hesitated, while

26

a look of inexpressible anguish overspread his face, as a score of sacred memories flashed through his mind.

He had *not* been *called* to the pastorate of the Dom Evangelia. There was no church when he came. He was the founder, the father, and they were his children, born of the Spirit through his preaching. How could he leave them with no hope of ever seeing them again?

"March on!"

The order brought him back in a moment, and picking up his small pack, with his faithful wife at his side, he stepped into the street.

To Prison

Oh, what a change! Often had he walked down that same street as an honoured citizen. Now he was a culprit under guard. For some minutes no word was spoken. The street was in darkness and his heart was even darker. There seemed to be no star of hope to which he might cling. He saw nothing but exile and dreary Siberian prisons, lifelong separation from those he loved, and at the end—death. Oh, the horrors of it. How could he bear it?

Heavy at heart, sad and perplexed, he walked on and on. His wife had not yet spoken a word. Now she trudged along as in a dream at his side. Poor little thing! In a moment life had become a vacancy to her. What had she now to live for? Husband gone, gone for ever; a three-month-old baby to care for—how could she endure it? But surely it was not real! Some horrible nightmare must have visited her. She would awake presently and find that all was well. But no, here was her husband, and just behind them two policemen. It must be true. And she sobbed in a low undertone as she stumbled on.

"Jesus, tell me, oh, tell me why," at last cried the prisoner within his own heart. "Why must I be taken away? Please tell me."

And as though from the darkened sky above came the answer: "Let not your heart be troubled."

"Ah! thank God! 'Let not your heart be troubled.' Oh! it's all right." And then these words:

> *"When peace, like a river, attendeth my way,*
> *When sorrows like sea billows roll,*
> *Whatever my lot, Thou has taught me to say:*
> *It is well, it is well with my soul."*

"Cheer up, Barbara dear. It is all right. Go home and bring our baby up in the Lord. It's all right." He spoke with great conviction, a real joy surging through his heart. God had answered.

Smiling up at him through her tears, the brave little woman took courage at his words, knowing that if he said all was right it must be so.

They parted at the prison gate. Bending low, he kissed her for the last time, and a moment later the iron gate closed and separated them, as it seemed, forever.

"Where will I sleep?" inquired the prisoner, turning to the policeman.

The light of the lantern showed him three prisoners, filthy, and probably alive with vermin, lying on three cots. There were no other beds in the cell.

"With one of them," answered the officer gruffly.

For a moment his courage failed. Never had he slept in such dirt and with such companions before. Then he took courage.

"Lord," he cried, "You were crucified between two thieves and surely I can sleep between two."

Then the officer left the cell and he was alone in the company of thieves, perhaps murderers.

Presently the door opened and a soldier called him by name. He had not yet lain down.

"Follow me," was the command. And he found himself in the office.

"If you will sign these papers agreeing to go to Siberia at your own expense, you may have three days to settle up your business affairs."

Such was the offer. It did not take him long to write his name. God, he knew, had intervened. The church must have prayed steadily from the time of his arrest. And prayer had been answered.

Returning to his cell, he picked up his bundle and started back for the church.

Released

What it all meant he did not know, but convinced that God was working, he stepped along at a brisk pace, with a great joy bubbling in his heart.

After proceeding for some distance, he suddenly saw two men coming toward him. Their figures looked familiar and as they drew nearer he recognized them as his two leading deacons. Their heads were down. Neither was speaking. They appeared to be completely disheartened. Their steps were slow and heavy. And as they approached their pastor, whom they had not yet observed, he was vividly reminded of the two disciples on the way to Emmaus.

"Brethren, hallelujah! I'm back!"

With startled looks they stopped suddenly and stood gazing at the man before them. The next moment their faces whitened as they clasped hands in terror.

"A ghost!"

The words were not uttered aloud, but, as they confessed later, that was what each exclaimed in his heart. Pastor Malof had already read their thoughts.

"No! No, brethren!" he cried, coming closer. "It's I, your pastor."

They felt him, welcomed him, cried over him, and finally, one on either side, they escorted him back to the church. The people had not yet left. They were still praying.

Now there were two groups to see. Upstairs were his wife and baby, from whom he had so sadly parted but a few hours before, and the church, his spiritual children.

But before he had married he had had a very definite understanding.

"Barbara," he had said, "I want you to know what kind of a husband I am to be."

"Well, dear," Barbara had answered, "I would surely like you to tell me."

"Jesus," he had responded, "is to be Number One. God's work is to be number two. And you, Barbara, must be number three. Are you willing?"

"Basil," she had replied, "if you were not a Christian of that type I would not be willing to marry you."

And so, passing by the door that led to his wife and child, he entered the church where the people were still praying.

"Brothers and sisters," he exclaimed, "the Lord has brought me out of the prison house!"

They sprang to their feet, took one look of utter amazement at him, and then, like a pack of hungry wolves, with tears of joy streaming from their eyes, the brethren flung themselves on his neck, each seeking to find a place for the holy Russian kiss. Unable to await their turn, they kissed him on the cheeks, mouth, nose, forehead and ears, and even on the top of his head and the back of his neck, while the sisters were standing modestly aside. It was the sweetest kissing match he had ever had.

Oh, the joy as they welcomed him back, as it were, from the dead! It seemed as though the separation had lasted for years. Pastor and people were again united, for a time at least.

Two days later by special decree of the Czar's Cabinet, in answer to the pastor's appeal, the sentence to Siberian exile was changed to banishment abroad. Thus by way of Sweden he came to the United States, where a great work was accomplished for Russian war prisoners, and, later, the Russian missionary movement organized. Thus the devil banished one preacher and the Lord sent back an army in his place. Basil Malof had heard and answered the Cry of the World.

CHAPTER II

IF YOU want to find countries where there is little or no poverty and much prosperity, you will have to go to Christian countries. In non-Christian lands the lot of the masses is indescribable poverty, and the virtual absence of prosperity.

If you want to find countries where there are hospitals to care for the sick, homes for the aged and orphanages for the helpless, again you will have to go to Christian countries. In non-Christian lands there are few, if any, hospitals or orphanages except those provided by Christian missionaries and no provision for the aged.

If you want to visit countries where people live in houses and where beggars do not clutter the streets, you will have to visit Christian countries. In non-Christian countries multitudes live in caves and shelters made out of old cans and boxes or in crowded river boats and beggars in their rags and nakedness throng the roads.

If you want to see countries where individuals own their own homes, and where they get three square meals a day, once again you will have to turn your eyes toward Christian countries. In non-Christian lands countless multitudes are destitute. They lack even the common necessities of life. They sleep on the street without enough cover to warm their bodies, and all their lives they are dependent on others. Even in Communistic countries men cannot forge ahead and freedom is unknown, for they live as slaves of an atheistic, dictatorial government that holds life cheap and knows no mercy.

If you enjoy a country where there are schools, universities and colleges, where the courts administer justice, you will have to live in a Christian country. In non-Christian lands the masses have no opportunity of getting an education and justice is unknown, for bribery is rampant.

If you love a country where women are equal to men and where hard manual labour is not the lot of the weaker sex, and where woman can take her place in the office and even in politics, you will have to seek a Christian country. In non-Christian lands woman is the slave of man. She may be one of several wives or concubines. She is illiterate. In many such countries she is seldom seen, even when parades are going by, for it is the men who stand and watch, not the women.

Christ Makes the Difference

What has made the difference? Christianity. Who has made the difference? Christ. Only in the countries that have been influenced by the teaching of Jesus is this difference found. Where Christ has gone, hospitals, schools, orphanages, leper asylums, homes for the blind, nurses and doctors have appeared. Where Christ has gone prosperity and plenty have followed. Where Christ has gone beggars have disappeared, homes have been built and the comforts of life have come. Where Christ has gone law has taken over and justice has been exercised. Where Christ has gone woman has been exalted, educated, reverenced and loved. Christian marriage has taken the place of polygamy. Where Christ has gone life is sacred and property protected, the individual given an opportunity to develop his business and to prosper, so that he can care for his family and leave something for them to inherit.

Go to a non-Christian land and you will find people hungry. Millions of them get only one meal a day or less and that a bowl of rice; they never know what it is to be satisfied. That is why there are so few fat people in non-Christian lands. They are thin for lack of nourishment. That is why they beg for a morsel of food. They are hungry. They have always been hungry and they always will be, for pagan governments are not much interested in their people's welfare.

Most people in Christian countries do not know what it is to be hungry. They have more than enough. The United States throws away sufficient food to feed a nation. God has given America and Canada a super-abundance of everything. The nation that recognizes Christ is rich. In 3 John 2 we are told that it is the will of God that His people should prosper. The greatest prosperity the world has ever seen will be during the Millennium and it will be because Jesus Christ will be exalted as Lord of lords and King of kings.

What about the heathen? If Christianity makes such a difference, then ought we not to tell them about Christ?

34

Their own religion cannot save them. They have never bettered their lot. Only Christianity can raise them from their degradation and filth to prosperity and righteousness. Only Christ can change their condition. Then why not give them Christ? He died for them. They have no other hope. All the by-products of Christianity will be theirs once they know Christ. Let us send out missionaries. Let us distribute the printed page. Let us get the message to them. By some means let us "Go . . . into all the world and preach the gospel".

One Church's Programme

The Peoples Church, Toronto, Canada, of which I was pastor, has contributed 4½ million dollars for missionary work, most of it for foreign work. At the present time we are giving seven times as much to missions as we spend on ourselves. For instance, last year we spent $45,000.00 on ourselves in Toronto and during the same period we sent $298,000.00 to the regions beyond. Thus we are trying to put missions first. At the present time we are contributing toward the support of some 350 missionaries on forty foreign fields under thirty-five accredited faith missionary societies.

Each year we hold a missionary convention that lasts for four weeks and five Sundays. There is no period of the year when the attendance is as large as it is during this convention. On Sundays we hold four services—one at eleven o'clock in the morning, one at three in the afternoon, one at seven in the evening and another at 9 p.m. As a rule some 2,000 people attend each of these services, making a total of 8,000 people for the entire Sunday. This continues for five Sundays.

We bring missionaries from various parts of the world, invite missionary leaders to speak on their work and show pictures, until our people catch such a vision that they can hardly wait for Sunday to make their investment for missions. Everyone takes part in the convention. They do not give cash. They make a faith-promise offering, agreeing to send in so much each month for the next twelve months. A pledge-offering is, of course, between the individual and the church, and the officials may be sent to collect it, but a faith-promise offering is between the individual and God, and the individual is never asked for it. He makes it to God and he deals with God alone. As a rule much more is received than the amount promised.

It is like buying on credit. If we had to pay cash we could not get what we want, but by signing a contract and agreeing to pay so much a week or month it is possible to obtain things that are beyond our reach otherwise. So it is with missions. We sign a contract with God and we agree to send in so much month by month for a year. Thus we receive sufficient to carry on our great missionary work.

Built on a Vision

The Peoples Church is built on a vision—the vision of getting the message to the Christless masses in the regions beyond. It is that alone which binds our people together. We have never had a split of any kind in the history of the church. Our people realize that "the supreme task of the church is the evangelization of the world" and they put missions first.

We have seen the same thing in dozens of other churches in the United States and Canada. It was my privilege to conduct the first convention ever held in Park Street Church, Boston. That church was then giving $3,200.00 a year to missions; it is now giving over $250,000.00 a year. For six years in succession I conducted their convention. The same thing happened in Grace Chapel, Philadelphia. That church was giving about $8,000.00 a year for missions. I held a convention there for five consecutive years. The Chapel is now giving over $100,000.00 each year. I have seen it happen in Presbyterian churches, Congregational churches, Baptist churches, Pentecostal churches, Independent churches, all kinds of churches. I have never known it to fail. God's plan is the convention. With a convention and a faith-promise offering, missions can be supported.

A Motto for Missions

About a quarter of a century ago God gave me a motto, which I put in the form of a question: "Why should anyone hear the Gospel twice before everyone has heard it once? I have used that motto all over the world and God has greatly blessed it. Missionary leaders everywhere are using it today. I have no objection to people hearing the Gospel a thousand times, but I do object when a pastor gives it to the same people for a quarter of a century and never once turns to those who have not yet heard. "The mission of the Church is missions", "This generation can only reach this generation", "You must go or send a substitute", "If God wills the evangelization of the world and you do not support missions, then you are opposed to the will of God"—these are some of the mottoes that influence us in our missionary work.

We must decide whether we are going to put our money into buildings or into the message. Jehovah's Witnesses build Kingdom Halls, not luxurious in any sense of the word. They know that the message is more important than the building. They do not build a beautiful church and invite the people to come in; they put their money into the message, the printed page, and send it out. At one of their services they baptized 7,136 converts, every one of them won by the printed page. The Communists are doing the same. They can even boast that they took China by means of the printed page. The Church of Jesus Christ is going to have to change its methods. The message is more important than the building.

Our people do not give as the world gives; namely, out of sympathy. We know that anyone will respond to physical needs. We have taught our people to give in order to carry out God's programme, which is to evangelize the unevangelized tribes of earth and thus bring back the King. Our policy is: "To hasten the return of our Lord by following His programme for this age, which is to 'preach the Gospel in all the world for a witness to all nations', and 'to take out a people for his name'. Our aim is to work among peoples, tribes and nations where Christ is not named."

Just One Job

When Jesus left this world he left us one job and one only—world evangelization. Everything else is of secondary importance. We have no women's missionary society in our church because we place the responsibility of missions upon everyone. It is only when the most important work of the church is given to everyone in the church that the church will indeed be a missionary church. I would never dream of giving the most important work of the church to any of the many societies in the church. I give it to the entire church.

We have 144 elders. Last year our elders gave $50,000.00 to missions. No one becomes an official in The Peoples Church unless he is backing the great work of world evangelization, and if he ever ceases to back that work he ceases to be an official. We have a choir of about seventy members. Last year our choir gave $14,000.00 to missions. We have a very small Sunday School. There are less than 500 in it and yet our Sunday School gave $52,000.00 to missions last year. We have a small group of business girls—about forty or fifty—and they gave over $5,000.00. Thus we have trained our people to put missions first. Any church can do the same.

There are still some 2,000 tribes without the Gospel, 2,000 languages into which no part of the Word of God has yet been translated. Jesus Christ cannot come to reign in millennial splendour, power, and glory until these tribes have been reached, for there must be some in the Body of Christ from every tribe, tongue and nation throughout the world. During the last twenty years some 500 new tribes have been evangelized. But when are we going to complete the task? When will we take Him seriously? When will we invest more in missions than we invest at home? When will we put missions first? I believe we can reach the remaining 2,000 tribes in the next twenty years, if we will.

I have been preaching the Gospel now for fifty years, but I am a pastor second, a missionary first. I am a hymn-writer and an author second, but a missionary first. I am an evangelist second, a missionary first. "The Gospel must first be published among all nations." God help us to accept the challenge and evangelize the world that the King may come back and reign.

CHAPTER III

FIRST THINGS FIRST

NEVER will I forget the appeal Sir Winston Churchill, then Prime Minister of Great Britain, made to the American people before they entered the war. It still rings in my ears. "Give us the tools and we'll finish the job." That's what our missionaries are saying today. They can distribute salvation booklets from door to door even before they learn the language. Then let us put the tools in their hands. No soldier should be sent out without proper equipment.

The Building or the Message

We must decide whether we are going to put our money into the building or into the Message. For nearly 1,900 years now the Church has been putting its money into the Building, and instead of getting out the message we have been erecting magnificent cathedrals and luxurious auditoriums in which to worship God. Jehovah's Witnesses have been much wiser. They put their money into the Message. They know that the Message is more important than the building. Yet all over the United States of America and the Dominion of Canada we are still investing in bricks and mortar, whereas God wants us to get out the Message.

Not until the Church realizes that the Message is more important than the building will we be able to evangelize the world. If for every fourteen cents invested in the "printed page" we can win a soul to Christ, then by all means we should put our money into the Message. God did not tell us to build luxurious churches and invite the people to come in. He told us to go out with the Message and preach the Gospel to the entire world. Let us then change our methods. Let us put our money not into the building but into the Message.

Equipment

I think we make a great mistake when we equip our missionaries as we sometimes do for their first term of service. We should wait until they have proved themselves. We should be sure that they will go back for the second term. That was the way it was with the great pioneers of the past. Some of them went out with just what they could carry in their two hands, and made good. Perhaps that is what made them pioneers. I think of one who stayed for twenty years without a furlough, and another who stayed for thirty years.

To give our missionaries large refrigerators, trucks, and all the other equipment that they are getting, during their first term of service on the field, is not a wise policy. When the time comes for them to return for their second term, then they may perhaps be able to take a few of the luxuries of life back with them. But during the first term we should be most cautious. Perhaps if they were to take just the bare necessities they would do a better job for

God. Rev. Tommie Titcombe's outfit cost him $30.00 and was carried in one large suitcase, and yet Tommie Titcombe tamed savage tribes and did a terriffic work for God.

It is possible to live so far above the natives that we lose our influence altogether. The natives look upon such missionaries as multi-millionaires and they cannot reach them. Unless a missionary lives as near to the native as possible, it is doubtful if he is going to be able to win him for Christ. If he has everything and the native has nothing, the gulf will be too wide.

We should not even expect our missionaries to be kept on the standards of life in America, nor should we pay them on the basis of what they could earn had they remained at home. Every missionary should get sufficient to live on, but, since he does not go to the field for personal advantage or to make money, his allowance should be kept at a minimum and his needs should be as few as possible.

That may be why British missionaries have been so successful on some fields where Americans have failed. I know that the British workers do not have enough often-times, but I am also sure that the Americans very often have too much. There should be some kind of equality at least and no missionary should live so far above the native that he loses his influence.

Now if we could take all the money that we use for extras that are not necessities and put it into the work itself by giving the missionary the tools that he needs to do his job, something worthwhile would be accomplished. That is why World Literature Crusade is trying so hard to provide millions of copies of the printed page for the missionaries to systematically distribute from house to house on every field.

Ability or Needs

That is why we work with the so-called Faith Missions. They do not base allowances on ability; they base their allowances on needs. The plan has always been to provide for the bare necessities of their workers. They have never paid them according to their ability. No true missionary, of course, is in the work for what he can get out of it. If he is really called of God he does not work for money; he goes out to win souls to Christ.

I am thinking now of a great denomination with a property value of $300,000,000. During one year their income was $1,000,000 a day, and of that amount $60,000,000 was used for preachers' salaries. They have a membership of 8,000,000 and 20,000 churches with full-time pastors. Yet this multi-millionaire denomination only has a little more than 1,000 missionaries in the entire world. It takes twenty of their churches to support one missionary. In other words, there are 8,000 members to a single worker on the foreign field. What a tragedy! What a lack of vision! The work here at home assumes greater importance by far than anything that is being done abroad. Could any real Christian be satisfied with such a programme? How ashamed we should feel! Why, with such resources we should be able to evangelize the entire world in our generation. God grant that we may catch the Lord's vision. For, remember, our generation is the only generation of Christians that can evangelize our generation of heathen.

Seven Times as Much

Most of our churches are spending more here at home than they are sending to the regions beyond. That shows that we consider the work at home of greater importance than the work in foreign lands. But is that right? I do not think so. That is why we reverse the order in The Peoples Church, Toronto. For every dollar we spend at home we send seven dollars to the foreign field. Last year, for instance, we spent $45,000.00 on ourselves here at home, but at the same time we invested $298,000.00 in missions—seven times as much—an average of $96.66 for each adherent for the year. We have done that consistently for the past twenty-eight years and we will continue doing it as long as there is a Peoples Church. The work in the foreign field must come first. All else is of secondary importance. During these past years in The Peoples Church we have seen $4\frac{1}{2}$ million dollars raised for foreign missionary work. Our people have caught the vision of world evangelization. They believe in putting first things first.

Then, too, we always emphasise spiritual rather than physical needs. Anyone will respond to physical needs, even the unsaved, but only born again Christians will be burdened about spiritual needs. The United Nations, through government agencies, are trying to meet the material needs of the world, but it is left to God's people to meet man's spiritual needs. Hence, when an appeal is made we always ask the question, "Is it a physical or a spiritual need?" We give our money for spiritual needs. Men are lost and perishing and they must be saved. Their greatest need is the Gospel. They need a Saviour.

One Thing

When the Lord Jesus Christ left this world, 1,900 years ago, He gave His disciples just one thing to do. He spoke in effect as follows: "I am leaving you now. I will be gone a long time, but one of these days I will return. Now, while I am absent there is just one thing I want you to do. I want you to take this Gospel of mine and give it to the entire world. See that every tribe, people, tongue and nation hears it. Do you understand? Then, when you have done it, I will be back, but not before." With these words He left them and they went to work. During the first generation they did a fine job. They succeeded in preaching His Gospel to most of the then known world. Of course they did not touch South America, North America, many of the islands of the seas, and vast parts of Europe, but they did go to most of the Roman world.

Then something happened. And now for nearly 1,900 years the Church of Jesus Christ has been doing a thousand and one things that Jesus never told the Church to do and has been neglecting the one and only thing He ever did tell the Church to do. We have not taken His Gospel to the entire world. We have built churches, seminaries, colleges, universities, hospitals. We have started Sunday-schools and Youth-for-Christ rallies. As a matter of fact we have done numerous things that we were never commanded to do, but we have failed to do the one thing that we were commanded to do. No wonder He has not returned. He is waiting for us to do what He told us to do during His absence.

Everything we have done has been good and abundantly worthwhile; but the trouble is, the good is always the enemy of the best. We should have kept before us our Lord's post-resurrection commands. We should have evangelized the world. Otherwise we have no ground for our existence as a church. There is no reason why we should have churches unless they are reaching out to those who have never heard. We must either go ourselves as missionaries or send out substitutes. Our Lord's post-resurrection commands were given to be obeyed. We must put first things first.

CHAPTER IV

WE MUST PROPAGATE THE GOSPEL

HOW are you going to propagate the Gospel if you refuse to pass it on to others? Will it not die with you? What if the Apostles had been satisfied to be saved themselves and had refused to take it to their fellow men? When they died, it too would have died. You and I would never have heard it. It would have perished in Palestine. The only reason we are Christians today is because they took it to others. If you and I keep it for ourselves it will die with us. God's plan is that we should proclaim it to those around us until at last all mankind will have heard it. What you keep spoils; what you sow bears fruit.

Suppose the Apostles had said, when Jesus told them to feed the five thousand: "Those back rows are too far away. We are weary and tired. These people in the front rows need to be fed. They, too, are hungry. Why leave them? We are having such a wonderful experience in feeding them that we should stay right here. We have no time to go back to the others." How, then, would the back rows have been fed? You know as well as I do that there was an absolutely equal distribution. They went to the back rows as well as the front rows. As a matter of fact no one in that entire multitude got a second helping

48

until everyone had had a first helping. Again I say, why should anyone hear the Gospel twice before everyone has heard it once? Why should anyone have two meals until everyone has had one meal? There should be an absolutely equal distribution.

Back Rows First

Do you know that not one pastor, not one church, not one Christian in 10,000 puts the back rows first. How do I know? I look at the financial report. Nearly everyone puts the front rows first. Why, they do not even go fifty-fifty. They spend *more* on the front rows than they do on the back.

In The Peoples Church, Toronto, of which I was pastor for thirty years, we give seven times as much to the foreign field as we spend on ourselves at home. For every dollar we spend at home we spend seven dollars in the regions beyond. We put the back rows first. That is the way it should be. That is the way it will be if we work according to God's plan.

A very wealthy man was sitting in his pew, but as the collection plate came along he indicated to the usher that it was not his practice to give anything. "Then," said the usher, "put in your hand and help yourself. This money is for the heathen." My friend, the man who does not give, identifies himself with the heathen. He is what they are. He believes in keeping everything for himself. If we were all to do that Christianity would die. We must propagate the Gospel.

Paul said: "I am debtor." He did not preach just to

get a reward. He preached because he had to preach. He said: "Woe is unto me if I preach not the Gospel." He had a debt to pay. Have you? Do you owe the heathen the Gospel? God says you do. Then you have a debt. Have you paid it? Are you paying it? The Bible says, "Owe no man anything." What we owe we should pay. The Gospel belongs to them. Then let us give it to them.

Just to show how much greater the need is in the foreign field than at home, I am going to give some statistics. Do you realize that in Africa there are fifty-six missionaries for each million, and in South America thirty missionaries to a million. In Korea there are only twenty to a million, and in Latin America nineteen. Then, when we turn to Japan, we find only fourteen missionaries to a million people, and in all India and Pakistan only nine, while in Indo-China there are about three. Now compare this, if you will, with the number of ministers in the United States. Will you believe me when I tell you that there are no less than 1,448 ministers of the Gospel to each million in America? What a contrast! What a difference! Is it right that there should be so many in the United States and so few in the other countries of the world? No wonder we stress missions, and especially foreign missions.

Our Lord's Vision

God had an only Son and He made Him a missionary. Then when Jesus came to this world He prayed: "As thou hast sent me into the world, even so have I also sent them into the world" (John 17: 18). He was a missionary, and we, too, must be missionaries. Just as the Father sent Him, so He sends us. We are to take His Gospel to the entire world. Never once did He become a pastor. Never once did He settle down in any one locality. Jesus was always travelling. He was continually on the go. In Matthew 9: 35 we read: "And Jesus went about all the cities and villages." He was ever thinking of the next villages and the next cities. He was going on and on to those who had never heard.

That is His vision for us. We are to take His Gospel to every tribe, tongue and nation throughout the entire world. Peter, you remember, thought the Gospel was only for the Jews, and God had to give him a special vision so that he would go to the household of Cornelius. God had to show him that the Gospel was for the Gentiles too. Even in our day it is difficult to get Christians to realize that the Gospel is for the whole world. Yet in almost every place where the great commission is mentioned, especially after His resurrection, it is made clear that all mankind is included.

Jesus showed us how it was to be done. First of all He sent out the twelve and then the seventy. He sent them out two by two. That is the way He wants us to go today. We should never go alone. Moreover, He endued them with power. They did not work in their own strength. For anyone to attempt to carry on missionary work in the energy of the flesh is foolhardy. The task is too great, the foes too many. The only way it is possible to succeed is by means of the power of the Spirit of God, the power available to each and every one of us.

Opposition and Persecution

Then, too, we must expect opposition and persecution. Jesus warned us that there would be persecution. In fact, He told His followers that some of them would be martyred. Yet, in spite of all the difficulties, He bade them go. There are very few fields where Satan will give up his territory without a struggle. The blood of the martyrs is still the seed of the Church. But it is on the fields where there has been the most persecution that the largest number of converts has been won. Think, if you will, of Ethiopia. How they were persecuted! How they were martyred! How they suffered for Christ! Yet Ethiopia has been one of the most fruitful fields. Tens of thousands are now rejoicing in God's salvation. Wherever Satan is working, God, too, is working. And the opposite is also true, for where God is working, there, too, Satan works. We must expect opposition.

Never have I read of such diabolical torture, persecution and martyrdom, as in Colombia during the past few years. It makes the blood run cold to hear about it. How the Christians have suffered! But it is always so where Rome holds sway. Whether in Colombia or Spain it is the same, for the Purple Curtain is no better than the Iron and the Bamboo Curtains. Freedom is unknown. Already eighty martyrs have sealed their testimony with their blood.

Nevertheless, in spite of persecution we must propagate the Gospel. We are obligated to give it to others, for unless we do, as I have already stated, it will die with us.

WE MUST PROPAGATE THE GOSPEL

The back rows must be fed. I appeal, therefore, to Christians everywhere to do everything possible to get out the Gospel message. Let us propagate it by word of mouth, by radio, transcription, loud-speakers, and the printed page, but let us propagate it, for only as we do so will the world be evangelized.

Why the Foreign Field?

There are those who tell us that the need is just as great at home as it is abroad. Suppose, for the sake of argument, we admit that it is, what then is the difference? At home the Gospel is available; abroad it is not. Those who want to hear it at home can hear it, whereas in foreign lands people cannot hear it even if they want to; it is not available.

In Mark 1: 37-38 Jesus refused to go back to those to whom He had preached the day before. Instead He said: "Let us go into the next towns, that I may preach there also: for therefore came I forth." Those He had preached to the day before had had their chance. Now He was going to give those who had not yet had an opportunity a chance. Paul, you remember, deliberately turned from the Jews to the Gentiles. He had given them their chance and they had rejected his message; hence, after preaching to them twice only, he turned his back on them and went to the Gentiles, to those who had not yet had an opportunity.

It seems to me that we waste a lot of money forcing the Gospel on those who have rejected it and who do not want it, whereas we should be investing our money to get the message to those who have never yet heard it; at least we should make it available to them. They, too, should have a chance.

At the present time the complete Bible is in only 207 languages. The New Testament alone is in 267 languages. There is at least one Gospel in 623 different languages. Others, of course, are in preparation and will soon be published, but there are 2,000 language groups in which there is no portion of God's Word at present. However, these 2,000 groups represent 5 per cent of the earth's population. In other words, there is some portion of the Word of God now available to 95 per cent of the total population of the world. It is now up to us to reach the remaining 5 per cent, which comprises some 2,000 different languages.

Then let us propagate the Gospel, and let us propagate it everywhere. Not just in our own little fence corner, but throughout the entire world. Let us take it to those who can read and to those who cannot, to the 95 per cent who have a written language, and to the 5 per cent who do not. Let us go to every tribe, tongue, people and nation, for only thus can we carry out our Lord's orders and bring back the King.

CHAPTER V

GIVE YE THEM TO EAT

G OD is calling out a new kind of missionary. Because of the rising tide of nationalism all over the world, the ministry of the foreign missionary is becoming more and more limited. In the largest cities his best policy is to co-operate with the national churches. He will accomplish but little alone. National leadership is taking over in most countries.

However, there is an increasing opportunity for the missionary who will devote his life to the ministry of the printed page. He can put announcements in the newspapers of a foreign country and offer a book on salvation free-of-charge and he will get hundreds of replies. He can organize the national workers and send them from house to house with his books. He can conduct Bible Schools and train his students to do the job.

Too many denominations put money into brick and mortar, hospitals, seminaries, institutions of one kind and another, only to have them confiscated when the Communists come. It is the message, not the building, that counts. There are far too many beautiful churches and cathedrals in foreign lands. Buildings should always be adequate, but simple and inexpensive. Let us emphasize the message and we will get the Gospel to countless thousands.

THE CRY OF THE WORLD

We are ready to co-operate with anyone anywhere in the world who has the vision and will to do work. Our books are written for the masses. They make the way of salvation plain. Many are on the deeper life for Christians. They are written for world-wide distribution.

The Great Problem

However, the problem of distribution is still the great problem. The book stores can only reach the few who are interested enough to come in and buy, but they do not and cannot get the message to the Christless masses everywhere. We must find another agency. Book stores have to make a profit. We must sell our books at cost if we are going to get them out in large quantities, just enough to enable us to print new editions. If we only put them in the book stores a few people will take the trouble to come in and buy, but if we are going to get them out in hundreds of thousands and reach multitudes, who otherwise will never be reached, we must do something more.

There should be a book table in every church and the best books available on salvation and the deeper life should be announced and sold at every service. That is why some of our churches are large and strong. That is why their converts are protected from false cults. In The Peoples Church, Toronto, we have always had a bookstand and thousands of dollars' worth of literature has been sold, most of it at cost price. Thus our people have been established in the Christian faith.

We should organize our workers to go from door to door, just as Jehovah's Witnesses do, and place books in every family in the community. Either give them away or sell them at cost, but get them out. *The pen is mightier than the voice.* My writing ministry is far more important than my preaching ministry. It was the distribution of Martin Luther's books (not his preaching) that gave us the Reformation. It was John Wycliffe's Bible that set England free. It was Bunyan's *Pilgrim's Progress* and the King James Version of the Bible that changed Britain. No church can do a greater work than to circulate the printed page. We must put our money into the message—not into the building—if we are to do the job.

God has enabled me to write some twenty-four books and some of them have been translated into over twenty-five languages. More than a million copies have been sold. I am continually raising money to distribute them, either at cost price or free of charge. I do not depend upon the book stores to get them out. After twenty-five years' experience I have learned that they can do very little, for they can only sell a limited number, and they must be circulated in millions if the world is to be reached and evangelized. Book stores have their place, and I thank God for them, but my book ministry must never be commercialized; it must always be a missionary work.

He Works Through Us

Do you remember the feeding of the 5,000 and the 4,000? There was a great multitude. But today the multitude is even greater. A whole world is starving for the Bread of Life. Jesus had compassion on them. Compassion is not sympathy or pity. Compassion is love in action. Do you have compassion? If so, you will do something about it. He called His disciples. He always does. He could have satisfied them without their help. But He works through us. He wants you to feed the multitudes.

They excused themselves by pointing to the problems. They only had a few loaves and fishes. What could they do? The difficulties were too great. It was an impossible task. But He had said: "Give ye them to eat." His commands are His enablements. If He tells us to do it, then it can be done. "The Saviour can solve every problem. There is nothing too hard for Jesus. There is nothing that He cannot do." His command is still the same: "Give ye them to eat." Who are we to refuse? Why look at the problem? Why not look to Him?

He blessed and broke. He has blessed you all with the blessings of salvation. But has He broken you? When the atom was broken there was power. When you are broken there will be power. Only broken men can feed multitudes. He made them sit down in companies. Why? He was systematic. There must be an equal distribution of the food. Otherwise those nearest would get all and the others nothing. That is not His plan. He wants all to be fed. The whole world must hear the Gospel. Not just the front rows, but all. None must be omitted. Every tribe, tongue and nation must be reached. Therefore we must be systematic. Like Paul, we must go from home to home. We must go to "every creature".

One of the chief exponents of this method is the Founder and Director of World Literature Crusade. His particular emphasis is the use of the printed page in the Light of the Great Commission, viz: a systematic effort to place paper missionaries in every home so as to give a witness to every creature. He engages in a thorough follow-up Bible Study Correspondence Course programme with, as his goal, "fruit that shall remain". Missionaries of more than a hundred denominations and societies are co-operating in his "Every Home Crusades". He is not putting his money into bricks and mortar but in the Message.

Paul did not build home bases in Palestine first and establish churches in his homeland; he took the Gospel to the whole known world. There are multitudes to be fed, and we must feed them. Then let us put missions first and home work second. Jehovah's Witnesses build modest inexpensive halls and put the money into their message. In one meeting they baptized 7,136 converts, in another 1,100, all won by the printed page. The Seventh Day Adventists do the same. So, too, do the Communists. The world is becoming literate. A million a week learn to read for the first time. But what are they going to read? The multitudes are hungry. Are we going to send them away empty, or are we going to feed them? Our Master said: "Give ye them to eat." He can satisfy every one of them.

Campaigns in Foreign Cities

Let all the churches in every foreign city get together and hold great evangelistic, soul-winning campaigns in the largest auditoriums. Let them join hands. Only then can they advance. A little boy was lost. Hundreds searched in vain. At last they joined hands—1,000 of them—and walked across the fields. Soon he was found, but it was too late; he was dead. They had worked alone too long. Had they united sooner, they could have saved him.

During the autumn of 1957 I held eight great campaigns in South America. In Montevideo seventy-one churches joined hands and held the greatest meetings ever seen in the history of the city. Over 600 came to Christ in one week. Thousands were blessed and helped. The largest hall in the country, with its 8,500 seats, was taken. In Buenos Aires 300 churches co-operated in a place holding 25,000. It was packed to capacity and over 1,500 accepted Christ. It was the same in Sao Paulo, Curitiba, Rosario, Santiago and Lima. As many as 6,000 crowded into a building seating less than 4,000. Hundreds thronged the inquiry rooms. In the eight campaigns there were some 10,000 decisions, 4,500 of them first-time decisions for salvation. Mrs. E. Spitzer arranged them.

I saw it in Australia and New Zealand, in South Africa and Europe. I have seen it in scores of foreign cities. It always happens when there is a systematic effort and the pastors work together. It is God's plan. If the atheists of Russia were to invite me to hold a campaign in Moscow, and give me freedom to preach the Gospel, I would go under their auspices. No one denomination or missionary society can evangelize the world. Only as we join hands and work together can we complete the task and bring back the King. Let us then see the multitudes as Jesus saw them and give them the Gospel.

GIVE YE THEM TO EAT

Don't Go Alone

When you go, however, don't go alone. Go with a wife or a husband. If that is impossible, then go with a fellow-missionary. Go two by two. Do not even think of going by yourself. The ideal way is to get married and then leave within a month or two. Don't wait until a child is coming. That will greatly add to your difficulties.

You have no idea what you will be up against on the mission field. The temptations and discouragements can overcome the strongest. You are no match for them. Our Lord knew that when He sent His disciples out two by two. He never sent them alone. It is a mistake for any board to send a missionary out by himself. "Two are better than one . . . for, if they fall, the other will lift up his fellow; but woe to him that is alone when he falleth, for he hath not another to help him up . . . And if one prevail against him, two shall withstand him" (Eccles. 4: 9–12).

If, through the lust of the flesh, you fall, it will probably be because you are working alone. Your whole ministry may be wrecked because your board sent you out all by yourself. Many a heart-breaking experience could have been avoided had there been a companion. Even a Samson can be seduced. David conquered Goliath, but Bath-sheba conquered David.

Where There are No Witnesses

When you go, go to a field where there are no churches and no witnesses for Christ. Do not go to the big cities where there are many national churches and pastors who can preach better evangelistic sermons than you can. Do not go to start a new work that will cause friction and that may seem competitive. These great cities are not mission fields any more than New York and Chicago are. They have had the Gospel for decades and they are filled with believers. All they need is evangelism.

If the world is to be evangelized you must go to tribes where Christ is not known. Paul always feared to build on another man's foundation. He headed for the regions beyond. Go, then, where there are no churches, no pastors, no Christians, and where there is no witness for Christ. When I go to the great cities I go to help the national churches, not to start a missionary work of my own. You are not a real missionary until you are working where no one else is working, at least no one except those in your mission. Thus, and thus only, can we evangelize the world and bring back the King. Our Lord is still saying: "Give ye them to eat."

CHAPTER VI

BRINGING BACK THE KING!

DO YOU know that only 9 per cent of the world's people speak English, and are you aware of the fact that 90 per cent of all Christians are working among this 9 per cent? What does that mean? It means that only 10 per cent of the Christians of the entire world are working among the 91 per cent who do not speak English. Is it right? Is it fair? Is it just? What must God think of us? Jesus told us to give the Gospel to the entire world, to every tongue and nation, and yet 90 per cent of us are concentrating on 9 per cent.

No wonder I emphasize my motto: "Why should anyone hear the Gospel twice before everyone has heard it once?" Note, if you will, that the question is not "Why should anyone hear the Gospel twice?" There is no question-mark at the end of the word "twice". You can give me a dozen reasons why the Gospel should be heard "twice". I can give you fifty. As a matter of fact, I have been preaching the Gospel to the same people in Toronto for over forty years now. That is as it should be. The question-mark, however, is at the end of the word "once" and the question is, why should I preach the Gospel of Jesus Christ to the people of Toronto for over forty years and never once turn to those who have not yet heard it for the first time? That is the meaning of my motto.

I am in favour of people hearing the message times without number, but I am not in favour of having it preached to the same people for years upon years without ever once turning to those who have not yet heard it. Why should we preach it again and again to the people at home and never once turn to those in foreign lands? God will surely hold us accountable. He has told us in unmistakable words that His Gospel is for the entire world. If we are giving it to the same people year after year and never once giving it to those who have not yet heard, then we are disobeying His post-resurrection commands. I simply use the word "twice" to emphasize the importance of giving God's Gospel to others. Many a pastor ministers to the same congregation all his life and ignores those who have never heard. Is it right? Most certainly such a ministry does not characterize the spirit of the New Testament. God's Gospel is for the whole world.

Some From Every Tribe

The Bible tells us that there must be some in the body of Christ from every tribe, tongue, nation and people. Not one must be missing. Every language must be represented. Yet there are still nearly 2,000 tribes that have not yet heard. There are no representatives of those tribes in the Church of Jesus Christ. God's programme has not yet been carried out. We have not reached the consummation of the Age. God has a definite plan. That plan

must be completed. Jesus spoke not of the end of the
world but of "the consummation of the Age". God's programme will not be carried out until we have won souls
to Jesus Christ from the last unreached tribe of earth.
Only then can He return and establish His kingdom.

How dare we ignore Mark 13: 10 and Matthew 24: 14!
Jesus says in effect: "The Gospel must first be published
among all nations . . . and then shall the end come."
How could He speak any clearer? He tells us that His
Gospel will have to be published among all the nations
of the world before "the consummation of the Age". He
is to return and establish His Kingdom here upon earth.
He Himself is to take over the reins of government and
rule in millennial splendour, power and glory for a thousand years. He is the legal Successor to David's throne,
and one of these days He is going to occupy that throne,
according to the predictions of God's Word. What is it,
then, that delays His Coming? It is the disobedience of
His Church. As long as 90 per cent of us concentrate on
9 per cent of earth's population the world will never be
evangelized. We must go to those who have never heard
if we are going to carry out God's programme.

Hasten His Coming

The question that the Bible asks is this: "Why speak
ye not a word of bringing the King back?" Then in
2 Peter 3: 12 we have the statement: "Looking for and
hasting unto the coming of the Day of God." Or, as it
is in the original, "hastening the coming". Is it then possible to bring back the King? Is it possible to hasten the

day when Jesus Christ will return? I believe it is. Had we evangelized the world five hundred years ago, He could have come back five hundred years ago. If we evangelize the world in this generation, He can come back in this generation. Everything depends on our obedience. We can hasten His coming by giving His Gospel to every tribe, tongue, people and nation. When I say "evangelize" I do not mean "Christianize". We are never told to Christianize the world, but we are told to *evangelize* the world.

Every prophetic Bible Conference should reach out to "the uttermost part of the earth". Money should be raised for the evangelization of the world. Plans should be laid for the reaching of the remaining unreached tribes. The greatest incentive to missions is the Second Coming of Christ. When we have carried out His orders He will be back.

The Work of the Church

Many people think that the Jews are to evangelize the world during the Tribulation. But the Jews have no Gospel. Moreover, if they are not to be saved until Christ returns in glory, they will not become Christians themselves until the close of the Tribulation. If the Holy Spirit goes with the Church, then how are men to be saved? But is it only the last generation in which God is interested? Paul tried to win those of his own generation.

Is the Church to be relieved of all responsibility? Have we been doing wrong in taking the Gospel to foreign lands during the last two centuries? Why were the past generations of Gentiles evangelized if God's plan is that only the final generation should be evangelized? What right have we to evangelize them if the Jews are to evangelize them? If I believed that, I would take my ease and do nothing. What utter nonsense! Of course the Church is responsible. If we want Christ to return we must carry out His post-resurrection commands. Then let us get to our task and evangelize the world.

Mark 13: 10 is not only a command, it is a prediction. The day will surely come when the Gospel of Jesus Christ will have been preached throughout the entire world. But it is perfectly clear from the use of the word "first" that something remains to be done *before* the End. There is a programme to be carried out. That programme is the evangelization of the world. As long as one nation has not had the Gospel the programme has not been completed. When the last nation gets the Gospel and there are some in the body of Christ from every nation, tongue and people, then, and then only, will God's plan be consummated. Only then can the Age end and Jesus Christ return to take over the reins of government. Therefore it is of paramount importance that we put forth every effort to evangelize the world.

Think, if you will, of our greatest missionary advocates: men like George Mueller of Bristol fame; Dr. A. B. Simpson, Founder and President of the Christian and Missionary Alliance; Dr. Henry W. Frost, Home Director of the China Inland Mission; Dr. Rowland V. Bingham, founder and General Director of the Sudan Interior Mission; Dan Crawford, and scores of others, who all believed in the programme of world evangelization as being completed before the consummation of the Age.

THE CRY OF THE WORLD

The Situation Today

Now what is the situation today? Earth's population numbers approximately 2,800,000,000. Of these only 800,000,000 call themselves Christian. That leaves 2,000,000,000 still in paganism. The Bible, or some portion of it, has yet to be translated into nearly 2,000 languages of the nearly 3,000 languages spoken today. Yet we concentrate on some 9 per cent of the total population of the world and ignore the 91 per cent. How can we do it? Our Lord's command is "Go ye into all the world". In which part of the field, then, are we to labour? God says: "The field is the world." If we do all our work in the United States of America we will be working in a fence corner. What about the rest of the field? Is it not God's plan that it, too, should be cultivated? Are we to work over and over again in one little fence corner and ignore the remaining part of the field? Are we not to evangelize the world?

America has had her chance. Canada has had an opportunity. Great Britain has not been overlooked. Ever since the advent of radio those who speak the English language can hear the Gospel if they want to; while out there in the darkness of heathenism there are but few radio-sending stations and receiving sets, so that they cannot hear even if they want to. Is it fair? Is it right? Why should so few hear the Gospel again and again while so many have never heard it once? Why should so few be fed time after time while so many have yet to have their first meal? What right have we to spend so much money on English literature when millions in the darkness of heathenism have nothing to read?

The supreme task of the Church is the evangelization of the world. There is nothing that we are doing here at home that is anything like as important as the work of getting the Gospel of Jesus Christ to those who have never heard it. Thousands of missionaries should be sent out. Millions of dollars should be contributed. Everything that the Church can do should be done if we are going to carry out God's plan and bring back the King.

CHAPTER VII

THE WOE OF GOD

"WOE is unto me, if I preach not" (1 Cor. 9: 16). The missionary goes to preach. That is his main business. He may have to do a little manual labour, but he ought not to waste his time any more than he has to. He should get the natives to do such work. His task is to preach the Gospel. He needs time for study and prayer, time for preparation, time to preach. He ought not to be occupied with other things. I used to work on my garden and lawn. I haven't done it now for years. My time is too valuable. I need every hour I can get for writing, editing, and sermon preparation.

That is one danger of Bible School work. Too many missionaries congregate at headquarters. Then they get on each other's nerves. Men who teach are apt to lie around all day Sunday doing nothing. They answered the Call in order to preach the Gospel on the mission field. They should take advantage of every opportunity. There are natives all around them who need to hear the Message. They should go out every Sunday, holding meetings, preaching, conducting campaigns, winning souls. I know that they feel the natives should do it and that their work is to train them. That is true. But let me tell you something. The natives will never do it unless the missionary sets the example.

"Woe is unto me if I preach not," exclaimed Paul. If your job is to preach, then preach. And don't let things of secondary importance turn you aside. The missionary who doesn't preach will soon dry up. He must give out if he is going to keep on fire. Don't let the natives have the joy of winning all the souls; you win some too. Don't just tell them how to do it, show them. Never forget that you have been called of God to preach.

"Woe is unto me if I preach not the gospel." In telling us to go, He told us to do one thing—preach the Gospel. We are not to stress education, medical work or social service, even though they all have their place. He does not tell us to give them our Western civilization. The societies that major in the by-products of Christianity oftentimes neglect the main issue. It is the Gospel that saves and nothing else. Therefore we must give them the Gospel. There are a lot of other things that they will get along with the Gospel, but first and foremost they must be given the Gospel itself. The by-products will follow in due time.

God chose the Jews to be a witness to the nations, but they failed Him. In Acts 1: 8 He tells us that we, too, are to be witnesses and that we are to witness world-wide. If we fail to witness, then we fail to carry out His programme. I wonder if we are doing what He expects us to do? Am I? Are you? Perhaps you are too old to go. Then you can send a substitute. You can back those who can go with your money. You can be a witness through another. You can invest in the printed page.

Are you going to fail your Lord and Master? Are you going to be a disappointment to Him? Or are you going to do what He told you to do? Are you going to be one of His witnesses? It is for you to decide.

Annual Giving per Member

It is most interesting to notice the per member contributions of various churches during the year. At least, it provides food for thought. It looks as though the richest denominations give the least. Here, then, is the annual giving per member as published by the National Council of the Churches of Christ in the U.S.A.

The Anglican Church of Canada	$ .23
Lutheran American	$1.06
Baptist: American Convention	$1.16
Disciples of Christ	$1.17
Methodist Church	$1.23
Congregational Christian	$1.40
Baptist Southern Convention	$1.44
Presbyterian in Canada	$1.50
Protestant Episcopal	$1.53
United Church of Canada	$1.60
Evangelical United Brethren	$1.81
Presbyterian U.S.A.	$2.28
Moravian Church (Northern Province)	$3.96
Reformed Church in America	$4.05
Baptist: Convention of Ontario and Quebec	$4.50
International Foursquare Gospel	$5.13
Methodist Wesleyan	$6.93

Church of the Nazarene	$7.27
Assemblies of God	$7.49
United Brethren in Christ . . .	$8.58
Mennonite General Conference . . .	$9.62
Evangelical Mission Covenant Church .	$9.69
Brethren in Christ	$12.13
Friends: Ohio Yearly Meeting . . .	$12.36
Methodist: Free	$12.77
Mennonite: Conference of Evangelicals .	$28.09

Contrast this with the Seventh Day Adventists, one of the false cults. They gave $32.78. What a rebuke! How much does your denomination give each year? How much does your church give? How much do you give? These figures show that, for the most part, there is little or no missionary vision and that the whole Church needs to be aroused.

Do you know that Russia and her satellites have done little or nothing for missions? The same is true of France, Spain and Portugal. Germany and the Scandinavian countries could have evangelized the world, and they have done something, at least; but higher criticism and ritualism have robbed them of their zeal, and only the evangelical forces in those countries have caught the vision. For many decades Great Britain has borne the burden of world evangelization and has done more than any other nation. I believe God gave Great Britain her many colonies in order to make possible their evangelization.

Today, however, there is only one country that can carry out the post-resurrection commands, and that country is the United States of America. The financial situation in the other countries of the world makes it impossible. The burden must now rest on Canada and the United States. America has all the money and all the young people needed. If America fails, then the world will not be evangelized; but I do not think America will fail. As I travel from the Atlantic to the Pacific, I am continually placing upon the hearts of American Christians the burden of world evangelization. America is the richest country on the face of the earth.

South Africa, I believe, alone could evangelize all of Africa, for South Africa has the money and the young people necessary. But will South Africa catch the vision? The Church in South India could evangelize the whole of India, and, being Indians, their missionaries could travel everywhere. But in all these years the Church of South India has not yet caught the vision. Therefore, I say, America is the only country in the entire world that we can look to. It, and it alone, has the resources necessary. It has the money and the men; now it must get the vision.

Catching the Vision

Thank God, many of the churches *are* catching the vision. We think of Park Street Congregational Church, Boston. At one time they only gave some $3,200.00 a year to missions. Now they are giving over $250,000.00. I had the privilege of conducting their Convention for six years and I saw the miracle take place. Grace Chapel in Philadelphia has done the same. When I held their first Convention they were giving less than $10,000.00 a year. Today they are giving over $100,000.00. I conducted their Convention for five years and I saw that miracle happen. In my travels across America I have seen dozens of churches increase their giving, until today they are contributing from $70,000.00 to $90,000.00 a year to missions.

I think of our own church—The Peoples Church—of which I have been pastor for thirty years. When I started my ministry the offering was only $3,500.00. Last year it was over $314,000.00. We are now giving seven times as much to missions as we are spending at home. For every dollar we spend on ourselves we send seven dollars to the foreign field. Our people have caught the missionary vision. We believe in putting first things first. Our church building is old, very old. It was built more than a hundred years ago, but we cannot afford to build a new one on account of our heavy obligations for the regions beyond. We must take care of our missionaries. They come first. We prefer to worship in a dilapidated building and send out more missionaries. Our Lord's post-resurrection commands must be carried out.

Moreover, our money is given for *foreign* missions: it is not given for benevolences. Benevolences can include anything from schools and colleges to ministers' pensions and manse construction and maintenance. It can include salaries for home workers and all kinds of overhead and administration expenses. In one denomination only 3 per cent of the money given for benevolences goes to Foreign Missions. We concentrate on *foreign* missions because so many churches emphasize *home* missions. The question

75

is not "How much does my church give to missions?" but "How much does it give to *foreign* missions?", namely world evangelization. What is it doing to bring back the King? How many unreached tribes is it reaching? It may be giving large sums to benevolences, but very little to *foreign* missions.

Making the Needs Known

In the early days there were some societies that felt it was wrong to make a direct appeal for money. They would not even allow their accepted candidates to tell of their needs and ask for funds. However, they had no hesitancy in asking for volunteers for the mission field and in appealing to young people to register their decision in a public way. For some reason they thought it was all right to ask for lives, but not for money. Apparently they were influenced by the policies of George Mueller rather than by the policies of the New Testament. The Apostle Paul, of course, had no hesitancy in making direct appeals. If it is right to ask for lives, it is right to ask for money. On the other hand, they were quite willing to have *churches* ask for money and then to accept the money received for the support of their missionary work.

I believe that God expects us to make our needs known and then to pray that He will lay it upon the hearts of people to meet them and trust Him to do so. There is plenty of room for faith even then. I know God can answer directly, as He did in the case of George Mueller and Hudson Taylor, and many others, but I believe that

76

the Scriptural policy is to make the needs known and appeal to God's people to meet those needs.

Of course, indirect appeals were constantly made. A great deal of deputational work was done. Magazines were published and, in many other ways, appeals were made, even though no offerings were taken. If we expect young men and women to stand up and offer themselves publicly for the foreign field, then we should expect those who cannot go to make just as public a decision regarding the support of those who can go and to do everything they can to send them.

Hence, I say: "Woe is unto me if I preach not the gospel." May that woe never be mine. May it never be yours. God help us to preach, and God help us to preach the Gospel. Preach it by word of mouth and also by the printed page. This world of ours must be evangelized. God has no other method. It is through "the foolishness of preaching" that men are to believe. Therefore let us go forth with the Gospel Message and preach it to men everywhere. "Woe is unto me if I preach not the gospel."

CHAPTER VIII

STILL THEY WAIT

MY first missionary work was among the Indians on the coast of British Columbia. I was only eighteen years of age, far too young to be a missionary. But the love of God burned in my heart and I was eager to do something for my Lord and Master. I lived alone in a mission house almost void of furniture. Never will I forget the loneliness and cold. I had to cut down my own firewood, saw it up, and prepare it for the stove. I cooked my own meals, mostly hardtack. During the week days I taught school and on Sundays I preached the Gospel to the Indians.

It was a trying experience, nearly 4,000 miles away from home. Sometimes, as I tramped through the great primeval forest surrounded by wild beasts, I lost the trail and, for awhile, wandered aimlessly trying to find it again. I suffered much, yet my heart was filled with unspeakable joy. Again and again I burst out in praise when my feet were so cold that they were numb. That was my first taste of missionary work. Since then I have gone to sixty-two countries.

In 1955 I travelled through South Africa, and after spending some three months in that country I journeyed from Cape Town in the south to Cairo in the north and on via Rome, Paris and London to my home in Toronto. These campaigns were arranged by Rev. Glyn Tudor.

Night after night I preached to large crowds during these African campaigns, and the power of the Lord was present. I saw more souls saved than ever before. In dozens, scores, and sometimes in hundreds, they walked down the aisles and stood at the front, later to go into the enquiry room, either to accept Christ as Saviour or as Victor, or to lay their lives on the altar as volunteers for the mission field. There were very close to 7,000 decisions of one kind and another during the campaigns, and, as far as possible, they were dealt with by personal workers in the enquiry room. It was a time of real blessing and revival. Most of it was among the three million white people in the Dutch Reformed, Baptist, Methodist, and Presbyterian churches.

But what I want to mention now is the fact that as I travelled through native territory I was informed that only about 10 per cent of the people had been evangelized and that some 90 per cent still remained to be reached. Yet there are paved roads everywhere and these people live within easy access of civilization. I saw them with the white paint on their faces and the charms around their necks. I saw them wearing heavy bracelets on their arms and legs, as well as around their necks and bodies. I saw them in their superstition and sin, and I wondered why the churches of South Africa had not evangelized them long ago.

The natives are being brought in from the far interior to work in the gold mines, and they told me that 1,000 come and 1,000 go every day. There are tract societies that are doing everything possible to distribute tracts among them, making them the missionaries to carry the Message back to their own people. They live in large locations, where there is a great deal of sin—drunkenness, witchcraft, immorality, and even murder.

However, these very locations present a golden opportunity for the preaching of the Gospel of Jesus Christ. The missionary does not have to journey far to reach them. They are right there, thousands upon thousands of them, easily accessible. It is dangerous work and hard work, but it pays and it pays abundantly. I think of the Dorothea Mission and many other agencies that are striving to give them the Gospel.

Java

Then there are other territories that are strategic and should be considered important mission fields. I think of the island of Java with its 60,000,000 people. Hundreds upon hundreds of missionaries should be sent to Java at once, for it presents a real challenge. In fact, no stone should be left unturned for the evangelization of all Indonesia.

However, Java is only one of the many open doors. There are opportunities everywhere for the preaching of the Gospel. New Guinea, for instance, is another. There are at least 626 different languages in New Guinea. Who, I wonder, is going to give them the Word of God? Then there are the Aborigines in Central Australia who speak some 200 dialects. What a mission field! Hundreds of unreached tribes are waiting in the South Sea Islands, tribes that speak at least 521 different languages.

South America

Then, of course, there is South America. South America is a harvest field. It was my privilege, during the autumn of 1957, to hold eight great campaigns in the larger cities. For the first time in the history of South America the churches co-operated. For instance, in Montevideo 71 churches united in the campaign; in Santiago, 90 churches; and in Buenos Aires, 300 churches. Such a thing had never happened before. Then, too, the crowds were out of this world. In Buenos Aires, a city of 6,000,000 people or more, we saw audiences of 25,000. I preached for two weeks. It was the same in the other great cities of South America. The crowds came—and remember, most of the people are Roman Catholics.

The most amazing experience of all was to see them coming forward, when I gave the invitation, in hundreds upon hundreds, just as they do in the Billy Graham campaigns. There were nearly 10,000 decisions of one kind and another, and at least 4,500 first-time decisions for salvation. The personal workers were kept busy in the enquiry rooms. The newspapers gave a great deal of space and stated that they were the greatest united evangelistic campaigns ever held in the history of South America. The services in Buenos Aires were televised and sent all across the country. Rev. Jack McAlister assisted me.

For years we have been sending missionaries to South America, and that is good, but we should have been sending evangelists. The only way to reach the great centres of population for Christ is by means of evangelism. What

F   81

happens in the country is seldom reported, but what happens in the city is known everywhere. Paul always headed for the great cities, knowing that if he could reach them the country would also be reached. He generally had an uproar. It is seldom that anything is accomplished until there is an uproar. People must start talking about the Gospel. That was what happened in our campaigns. That is why I say that we should be sending our very finest evangelists—evangelists able to preach by interpretation—to South America, and in fact to all the great cities throughout the world. They can accomplish more there than they can ever accomplish here. We need evangelism in the foreign field. We must capture the cities for God.

After we left, the various churches did the follow-up work, in order to conserve the results. I did not hold my campaigns under the auspices of the missionaries; I held them under the auspices of the national churches, and that is the only way to have successful campaigns. The nationals must not be ignored. Moreover, all the expenses were met in each campaign and money left over. The national churches themselves covered everything, so that there was no lack. They were the greatest campaigns I have ever been privileged to hold. I trust that many evangelists will hear the call and go with the Gospel of Jesus Christ to the teeming millions in our great centres of population in foreign lands.

So much to do and so little time! God help us to do more than we have ever done before to get out the message and bring back the King.

Leave Early

May I say that if you are twenty-seven years of age you should get to the field as soon as possible. You can never accomplish much without the language, and if you want to speak the language like a native you should get it before you are thirty years of age. Any course of study that you can take in this country after you are thirty will never make up for the experience that you can get in the land to which God has called you as a missionary. You will be much more valuable without higher education if you have a good knowledge of the language than you would be with higher education, if you cannot speak the language fluently. Therefore I would urge you to leave for the field, if at all possible, when you are twenty-seven years of age, so that you can really master the language and preach the Gospel in the native tongue. You will find yourself deficient all your life, even though you have the highest possible education, if you are unable to speak fluently the language of the people among whom you work.

Our Missionary Mottoes

Perhaps if I were to give you some of my great missionary mottoes that I have used all over the United States and Canada, as well as in countries overseas, you would be inspired, even as others have been. I am not going to comment on them, I am just going to leave them with you and let you think them through. Suffice it to say that they have been used of God to challenge young people everywhere and to lead Christians of all denominations to give more for the spread of the Gospel in the regions beyond. They will speak to you, too, if you will let them.

During the days of our Annual Missionary Convention we put them up on the walls of our church so that the people can read them during the entire time that the Convention is being held, and they speak to many a heart. You, too, could use them in one way or another. I am sure God will make them a blessing if you do. Let me quote them one by one:

"You must go or send a substitute."—*Oswald J. Smith*.

"This generation can only reach this generation."

"The mission of the Church is missions."

"Anywhere, provided it be forward."—*David Livingstone*.

"Farther, still farther, into the night."

"If God wills the evangelization of the world, and you refuse to support missions, then you are opposed to the will of God."—*Oswald J. Smith*.

"Attempt great things for God, expect great things from God."—*Wm. Carey*.

"The church that does not evangelize will fossilize."

"Why should anyone hear the Gospel twice before everyone has heard it once."—*Oswald J. Smith*.

"You can't take it with you, but you can send it on ahead."—*Oswald J. Smith*.

"Only as the Church fulfils her missionary obligation does she justify her existence."

"A man may die leaving upwards of a million, without taking any of it upwards."—*Wm. Fetler*.

"The light that shines farthest shines brightest nearest home."

"If Jesus Christ be God and died for me, then no sacrifice can be too great for me to make for Him." —*C. T. Studd.*

"Give according to your income lest God make your income according to your giving."—*Oswald J. Smith.*

"The prospects are as bright as the promises of God." —*Judson.*

"The greatest foes of missions are prejudice and indifference, and ignorance is the mother of them both."

"Now let me burn out for God."—*Henry Martyn.*

"Yet more, O my God, more toil, more agony, more suffering for Thee."—*Francis Xavier.*

"We can give without loving, but we cannot love without giving."

"The church which ceases to be evangelistic will soon cease to be evangelical."—*Alexander Duff.*

"Not, how much of *my* money will I give to God, but, how much of God's money will I keep for myself?"

"The supreme task of the Church is the evangelization of the world."

"Untold millions are still untold."

"Oh for a hundred thousand lives to be spent in the service of Christ!"—*George Whitefield.*

"You have one business on earth—to save souls." —*John Wesley.*

"Sympathy is no substitute for action."

"Christ alone can save the world, but Christ cannot save the world alone."

CHAPTER IX

HOW CAN WE EVANGELIZE THE WORLD IN THIS GENERATION?

IF I were to choose a text I would turn to Mark 13: 10
—"The Gospel—The Gospel must—The Gospel must
first—The Gospel must first be published—The Gospel must first be published among all nations."

I wish I could spend at least half-an-hour on every one of these statements, for each one is of paramount importance, but I only have time to deal with one. As a matter of fact I am going to emphasize just one word, the word "published". "The Gospel must first be published among all nations."

I believe it is God's plan that every man should have the Gospel in his own tongue, and yet there are 2,000 languages into which no portion of the Word of God has as yet been translated. We have had it in our tongue from our earliest childhood. Why should they be denied?

Do you realize that you owe everything you are to the printed page? Had it not been for the Word of God you would not have been a Christian. The Bible says, "Faith cometh by hearing, and hearing by the Word of God". How then can we expect the heathen to hear and be saved if they do not even have it?

What was it that gave us the Reformation? You say it was Martin Luther's preaching. I do not believe it was.

86

HOW CAN WE EVANGELIZE THE WORLD?

Martin Luther wrote nearly 100 books and circulated them throughout Western Europe, and, as a result of the *writings* of Martin Luther, there came the Reformation. Where would you have been today if it had not been for the Reformation? The Dark Ages would still be upon us and you in all probability would be a Roman Catholic.

I believe that the greatest miracle of our day and generation is the increasing literacy around the world. Have you any idea as to how many people learn to read every week? Let me tell you. Three million people learn to read every seven days. What does that mean? It means that last week three million people who could not read one single word are able to read this week. It means that next week another three million people who cannot read a single word this week will be able to read next week. Three million people every week—one hundred and fifty million people a year.

That has never happened before in the 6,000 years of man's history on earth. Up until our generation only a handful of people have been able to read in comparison to the vast multitudes unable. But today the peoples of the world are learning to read.

The Communists have the Answer

But what are they going to read? The Communists have the answer. They know something of the power of the printed page.

Did you ever hear of a man by the name of Charles Darwin? Did you ever hear of a book he wrote called *The Origin of Species*? Do you realize that as the result of the writing of that one book your sons and daughters are being subjected to the theory—and I do not say the fact, for evolution has never been proven, it is still only a theory—to the theory of evolution in practically all the Universities, Colleges and High Schools of the world? Nothing has ever damaged the Word of God as has the theory of evolution. That gives you some idea of the influence of just one book.

Do you know that the Communists printed two pieces of literature in a single year for every man, every woman, every boy, and every girl, on the face of the earth? What other nation has done that? No other nation has, but the Communists have.

Why, they even boast of having taken China by means of the printed page. If, instead of building hospitals and educational institutions, we had put our money into the message in China, that country might never have gone behind the Bamboo Curtain. China could have been evangelized by the printed page.

For twenty-five years before the Russian Revolution the Communists poured their literature into Russia.

Some time ago the United Nations gave the number of different books printed by five of the leading nations of the world. Which nation do you think came first? Russia came first with 60,000 different titles. Which nation came second? The most literate nation on the face of the earth —Japan—with 24,000 titles. Great Britain came third with 19,000 and India fourth with 18,000. Which nation do you think came last of all? The United States of America. During that year America only printed 12,000 different titles. Now, tell me, which nation believes in the power of the printed page? The United States with 12,000 or Russia with 60,000?

HOW CAN WE EVANGELIZE THE WORLD?

Do you know that during one year Russia printed no less than one billion books and translated 5,000. During the same year the United States only translated 800 and Great Britain 600. Again I ask, Which nation believes in the power of the printed page?

Russia is out to win the minds of men by means of the printed page. You can buy Russian magazines on almost any news-stand in the United States of America and throughout the world. Russia may not need a war, not if she can win the cold war by using the printed page.

Ghandi's grandson—Ghandi of India—said the other day in Los Angeles, "The missionaries taught us to read, but the Communists gave us the books". Think of it, if you will. "The missionaries taught us to read, but the Communists gave us the books." Why didn't the missionaries give them the books? Because the churches that had sent out the missionaries had never caught the vision. They had failed to place the ammunition in the hands of their missionaries. So, after having taught the people to read, they allowed the Communists to come along and supply the reading material.

Jehovah's Witnesses are on the Job

Yes, and let me tell you something else, believe it or not, the False Cults are on the job.

Do you realize that Jehovah's Witnesses have the largest religious printing press in the world? Why is it that the Christian Church does not have the largest press? Simply because the Christian Church has never realized the value of literature. Do you know how many magazines that one press prints every minute? Every sixty seconds that one press produces 500 magazines (eighty-four million in a single year). Where are these magazines circulated? Through the English speaking world? Yes. But mainly in the Orient, Asia, Africa and South America.

Are Jehovah's Witnesses getting results? Does it pay to get out the printed page? Jehovah's Witnesses held a Baptismal Service in New York some time ago, where, at that one service they baptised 7,136 converts. How many has your church baptised? How many have all the churches of America baptised? How many were baptised on the Day of Pentecost? Less than half that number. And this is the point, every convert was won by the means of the printed page. Does it pay? Jehovah's Witnesses think it does.

Did you ever see the little inexpensive Kingdom Halls that Jehovah's Witnesses have? You have never known them to build a cathedral. Why? Because they realize that the message is more important than the building. Therefore, they put their money into the message, not into the building.

That is where the Christian Church has made its greatest mistake. We have been putting our money into buildings instead of the message. It is the message that is dynamite. "The Gospel is the power of God unto salvation." Not the building but the message.

In one year, according to the National Council of Churches, there were built in the United States of America, 6,000 new churches at a cost of one billion dollars. When I read that, I said to myself, "I wish I could somehow stop that building programme for just twelve months and get my hands on that Billion Dollars. If I could put that

Billion Dollars into the Message, this world, I believe, could be evangelized within a matter of years." Now I am not against building new churches. I think we ought to build adequately for our needs. But I am against building luxurious cathedrals when the world is so desperately in need of the message of God's salvation.

Do you know what one billion dollars would do? It would put a 16-page booklet, containing a complete Gospel message, in every home in the world and in thirty-five other worlds just like it.

How many church buildings were there when the Apostle Paul commenced his great missionary work? Not one. Yet we think we must have Home Bases before we can do anything. Paul went out before even a single church building had been erected.

My friends, we will have to decide whether we are going to put our money into the building or into the message if we are ever going to evangelize the world.

During a single year the Seventh Day Adventists invested $21,000,000 in the printed page in 218 languages. They, too, believe in the power of the message.

World Literature Crusade

That is why I became interested in World Literature Crusade. They are out to place the Gospel Message in every home in a given country, thus reaching every family and, ultimately, every creature with the Gospel. They do it in a systematic way so that no one will be overlooked.

The messages are not printed in America because they would then be foreign and, on account of the rising tide of nationalism, nothing foreign is acceptable.

They are printed in foreign countries—the country of distribution—because the work can be done so much cheaper, less than one-fifth the cost in America, and there is no money to waste.

If they are printed in America, there would be transportation and duty charges and these they want to avoid.

How much do the missionaries pay for them? Absolutely nothing. They get the literature free-of-charge. All they have to do is to agree not to miss a single home in their territory.

Do you know that 106 denominations and missionary societies are co-operating at the present time in these Every Home Crusades, practically all the evangelical movements of the world?

They are not printed in thousands, they are printed in millions. It is a world task and it requires a world vision.

Already the work has been finished in Japan. So far as we know, every home where 94 million people live has had a Gospel message. What has been the result? No less than 60,000 Japanese have written in asking to be enrolled in a Bible Correspondence Course, requesting more literature, or enquiring about the way of salvation.

Every home in South Korea, so far as we know, has had a Gospel Message. What has been the result there? No less than 70,000 Koreans have written in indicating their interest in the Gospel, requesting additional literature, and asking to be enrolled in a Bible Correspondence Course.

How could you get results like that in any other way? All the missionaries in a given country could not produce such results. The printed page is God's method for our day and generation.

HOW CAN WE EVANGELIZE THE WORLD?

In some areas it only costs 14¢ to win a soul to Jesus Christ by means of the printed page. That means that there is no cheaper way to carry on missionary work. If we can systematically put a copy of the printed page in every home in a country we will have reached "every creature" in that country, for we will have reached every member of the family. Our missionaries can organize a group of workers and send them from door to door, from house to house, with the message. That was Paul's method and therefore it is Scriptural. He evangelized from "house to house", so as to reach "every creature" with the Gospel message. We cannot do better than to follow his example.

Jesus said "every creature". The only way you can reach every creature is to reach every home and family. That cannot be done by sending out missionaries or by means of radio. The only way it can be done is by using the printed page. There is no other way that I know of to carry out our Lord's command.

Behind the Iron Curtain

My books are now in 35 different languages and we are putting them into more all the time. My gospel messages are going out in hundreds of thousands. I believe the work of tract distribution should be followed up with a booklet containing a Gospel Message.

Recently I had two books published in the Polish language in Warsaw, Poland, behind the Iron Curtain. That was a miracle. These are now being distributed all over Poland by the 280 churches that are still open. I do not write off a country simply because it goes behind the

Iron Curtain, the Bamboo or the Purple Curtain. If I cannot send in missionaries, I can send in the Gospel. The whole world must be evangelized.

Some time ago a certain Bible School sent its students out to a very busy street to give out gospel tracts on the sidewalk. Do you know what happened? Within ten minutes' time the whole of the street was simply littered with torn Gospel tracts. The people had taken them, had glanced at them, had seen that they were tracts, and then had torn them to pieces and thrown them away. That is how much the printed page is appreciated in America.

I have travelled all over foreign countries. I have given out gospel tracts everywhere. I have seen thousands upon thousands of tracts distributed. Do you know, I have never yet seen a native tear up a Gospel tract, or a Salvation booklet? When you hand a native in a foreign land a tract or a booklet, he will thank you for it most graciously, and then sit down right where he is—in the train or the bus or the street car—and read it unashamed. Literature is appreciated in foreign lands. That is why I am putting my money into "foreign literature" rather than into literature for this country.

On one of our Russian fields the Chairman called all the Pastors and Missionaries to the front, and taking one of my books in the Russian language, he tore it to pieces, after which he handed each Missionary and Pastor, just one page. That page was folded very carefully and put in an inside pocket and then taken back into the far Interior. There the missionary gathered the villagers around him and read it word for word, knowing nothing of what went before or what came after. It was read until many had memorized it. Where there is a famine of the Word it is treasured as gold.

"Give Us the Tools"

It was during the time of the last World War. France had fallen. The United States had not yet come in. Great Britain was standing alone with her back against the wall expecting almost instant invasion. Sir Winston Churchill, the Prime Minister, decided to speak directly to the American people. I was driving along the highway with my wife. I drew my car to the side and turned off the engine, so that I would not miss a word and then I tuned in London, England.

The Prime Minister only spoke for two or three minutes, but he said something that I have never forgotten from that day to this. Sir Winston Churchill, in speaking to the American people, said this: "Give us the tools and we will finish the job". From that day to this I have been going up and down the land, speaking to congregations of all denominations on behalf of our 42,250 Protestant missionaries, and I have been saying, "Give us the tools and we will finish the job."

That is what I say to you now. As fast as the money comes in the message goes out. We have the workers. We have the organization. All we need are the funds with which to do the work. Have you ever invested in the printed page? Have you ever given anything to get the message out? May God help you to do what you can. "Give us the tools and we will finish the job".

CHAPTER X

DOES THE ROMAN CATHOLIC CHURCH GO BACK TO THE APOSTLES?

THE Roman Catholic Church appeared for the first time in the fifth century. For the first four centuries Christians followed the teaching of the Apostles, as recorded in the New Testament. Then Roman Catholicism gradually took over and superseded the Bible, so that the Apostolic Church became the Roman Catholic Church. Gregory I (590–604) was the first pope. None of the Christians of the first four centuries were Roman Catholics, for there was no Roman Catholic Church at that time.

When the fourth century ended, the churches were under the jurisdiction of five patriarchs of equal authority. Finally there were just two—the one in Rome and the one in Constantinople. The word "pope" was first applied to Western bishops and it was not until A.D. 500 that it was restricted to the Bishop of Rome, who sought to be recognized as the universal bishop of the Church. That claim, however, was never accepted by the whole Church.

It was natural, perhaps, that the Church, founded during the days of the Roman Empire, should finally accept that form of government and become the autocratic organization that it has, and be ruled from the top by a pope, but, as I have already stated, it did not happen all at once. It was five hundred years before such a government appeared and before the Roman Catholic Church existed.

The First Pope

Roman Catholicism tells us that Peter was the first pope and that he resided in Rome. That is pure fiction. There is not the slightest evidence that Peter ever saw Rome. Most certainly Peter made no such claim for himself or his successors. In fact he spoke against "lording it over God's flock" (1 Pet. 5: 3).

Pope Leo I (440–61) was the first to proclaim himself head of the whole Church. However, the Council of Chalcedon (451), which was the Fourth Ecumenical Council, granted the Patriarch of Constantinople equal prerogatives and did not recognize the Patriarch of Rome as his superior.

Gregory I (590–604), as I have stated, is recognized as the very first real pope of the Roman Catholic Church. When the Patriarch of Constantinople declared that he himself was the universal bishop, Gregory was greatly aggravated. He refused to recognize him and would not allow the term to be applied to himself. However, the West grew stronger and stronger and the East weaker and weaker, until, at last, well after A.D. 500, the Bishop of Rome came to be recognized as pope by the Western Church. Boniface III (A.D. 607) was the first to get the title "universal bishop".

Charlemagne, under Pope Leo III (795–816), was the ruler who brought the Papacy to its position as a world power. Nicholas I (858–867) through the forgeries of ancient historical documents made it appear that the Papacy had been unchanging from the beginning. These documents were proven to be spurious a few centuries later. They have been spoken of as "the most colossal literary fraud in history". However, they supported the Papacy more than any other agency.

The Dark Ages

So far did the popes of Rome depart from the teachings of Jesus and Paul that the Dark Ages set in and for a thousand years the paganism of Roman Catholicism was in control. The Church and not the Bible became the supreme authority. Christians who held to the teachings of Christ were considered heretics and were bitterly persecuted. At least fifty million of them perished by torture and death at the hands of Rome. Whereas Christ and his Apostles taught salvation by faith, Rome introduced salvation by works. Church councils proclaimed doctrines and dogmas utterly contrary to the Word of God. The Dark Ages continued until God raised up Martin Luther to combat the errors of Rome and restore the doctrines and practices of the early Church.

During the past three hundred years we have again, in the various evangelical denominations, the Church of the first four centuries. The darkness of Romanism has disappeared and the glorious light of the Gospel of Jesus Christ has burst forth. The Roman Catholic Church is not the Church Jesus Christ founded. Neither its doctrines nor its practices can be recognized in the New Testament.

THE ROMAN CATHOLIC CHURCH

The Church founded by Christ and His Apostles, and especially by Paul, is the Church of all the evangelicals of all denominations that believe and teach the Bible and proclaim salvation without money and without price. On this tremendous truth it is bound together regardless of its differences on minor issues. "The Church's one foundation is Jesus Christ her Lord." Not Peter, but Christ. All are one in Him regardless of denominational affiliation. The Roman Catholic Church, on the other hand, has betrayed the Faith, trampled underfoot the great doctrines of grace, and condemned as heretics the true followers of the Saviour.

The First Five Centuries

Few of the doctrines of the Roman Catholic Church were held by the Christians of the first five centuries, nor are they to be found in the New Testament Scriptures. No priest was forbidden to marry. There were no images in the churches. Mass was unknown. There was no confessional and no purgatory. There were no prayers to Mary and no beads or rosaries. All were foreign both to the early Christians and the New Testament. The doctrines and practices of the New Testament were observed by the entire Christian Church and the New Testament was completed before the close of the first century. As a matter of fact, it was written by those who had lived in the days of Jesus and it was accepted as authoritative. Catholic belief, dogmas and practices were all invented later and are not to be found anywhere in the Bible. Paul's letters were accepted by Peter as Scripture long before they were passed down by a church council (2 Pet. 3: 2, 15–16).

It was A.D. 310 before prayers for the dead were said. It was A.D. 320 when wax candles were introduced. It was A.D. 375 before there was any worship of the saints and angels. Mass was not said until A.D. 394. There was no worship of the Virgin Mary until A.D. 431. The doctrine of Purgatory was first taught in A.D. 593. It was in A.D. 788 that the worship of images and relics was authorized. Celibacy for priests was decreed in A.D. 1074. Prayer Beads were not invented until A.D. 1090. Confession commenced in A.D. 1215. The Immaculate Conception of the Virgin Mary was decreed in A.D. 1854. It was not until A.D. 1870 that the pope was declared infallible. The Assumption of Mary was made a dogma in A.D. 1950.

That is why none of these doctrines can be found in the Bible. They were decreed by the Church. But it was A.D. 1545 before church tradition was placed on the same level as the Scriptures. Therefore, I say again, the Roman Catholic Church is not the Church of the New Testament. It is as different as day is from night. Nearly all of its dogmas were invented after the New Testament had been written and accepted as we now have it, and most of them from 400 to 500 years or more after Christ. I could give the dates—and they are very late—for all its other dogmas and practices, but the above will suffice.

The Bible Comes First

With Catholics the Church comes first and the Bible second; whereas with Evangelicals the Bible always comes first and is the final court of appeal. The Bible says: They "searched the scriptures daily, whether those things were so" (Acts 17: 11). Hence the Scriptures, not Peter, not the pope, not church leaders or councils, but the Old Testament Scriptures settled everything. Even the preaching of Paul—the greatest of all the Apostles— was tested by the Scriptures, according to Acts 17: 11. It was the common people and not the priests who searched the Scriptures.

What does the Bible say? Listen: "To the law and to the testimony: if they speak not according to this word, it is because there is no light in them" (Isa. 8: 20). The Bible, then, is the final word. It is not what the Church says but what the Scriptures say. Catholics do not believe that. They put the Church first, yet Peter based his first two sermons on the Bible.

"For I testify unto every man that heareth the words of the prophecy of this book, If any man shall add unto these things, God shall add unto him the plagues that are written in this book: And if any man shall take away from the words of the book of this prophecy, God shall take away his part out of the book of life, and out of the holy city, and from the things which are written in this book" (Rev. 22: 18, 19). The Catholic Church both adds and takes away. So it stands condemned (Deut. 4: 2).

The pope is infallible, say the Catholics. Which pope? I ask. Sometimes there were two and even three all claiming to be the pope and each denouncing the other. Which, I ask, is the true pope? Which was infallible? Have you read church history? Do you know that the Popes contradicted each other? Do you realise that the apostolic succession of Popes has been broken? Do you know about the awful sins of immorality, theft, and murder, committed by the popes from A.D. 904 to 1046? Could they have been infallible? Have you read church history, I say? If not, then before you disagree read it; read it for yourself. You will find the whole revolting record in *Halley's Bible Handbook,* twenty-second edition, page 882. It is shocking beyond words.

No, my friend, not the pope, not the Church, but the Bible. It alone is unchangeable. There is no other authority. Man, the Church and the pope errs. The Bible is God's infallible, inspired Word. "To the law and to the testimony," cried the prophet. "To the Bible," cries the Christian. That, I say, is where Protestants and Catholics differ. With the Catholics it is the Church, with the Protestants it is the Bible.

Let us always remember that the Roman Catholic Church does not date back to the days of the Apostles, and that it was not the first church; that Peter and Paul did not belong to it or, in fact, know anything about it, since it did not come into existence until the fifth century. The early Christian martyrs did not know it, and it can take no credit for them. None of the Christians in the catacombs of Rome were Roman Catholics.

Thank God for Martin Luther and the Reformation. Thank God for a man who had the courage to stand against the Pope and Emperor, that the masses might be emancipated from earth's most heartless tyrant. Had it not been for the Reformation mankind might never have been free from the shackles of Rome.

CHAPTER XI

AFTER THE CHILDREN ARE GONE

THERE are so many married couples today who are unhappy that I feel I must say something to both husbands and wives regarding the married relationship. Many there are who have come to me as a minister for advice. Very few seem to be perfectly satisfied, especially after the children are gone.

I believe that the most perfect relationship in life is the one of husband and wife. God Himself has ordained it so—one woman for one man and one man for one woman. Children then become the expression of that relationship, and so you have husband, wife and children—the perfect home.

Love is the bond that unites husband and wife, the one to the other. If there is love, then happiness is found in poverty and adversity. If it is absent, then there is no happiness in riches and prosperity. With love a house is a home; without it, it is nothing but a house.

Today divorce is on the increase, and for other than the one Bible reason. Wives and husbands are exchanged by legal procedure, so that multitudes are living in open adultery, and then we wonder why God does not bless our homes and our nation.

Should I Divorce Him?

What, you ask, am I to do when my husband is unfaithful to me? Should I divorce him? By no means. If he is penitent, if he comes to you and asks your pardon, then forgive him and take him back. Otherwise it will break your heart and wreck your home. Forgive him and never mention it to him again.

But if it becomes a habit with him and he does it again and again and you know he is living in sin with another woman, and if there is no repentance and he will not forsake it, then you will have no choice but to separate from him and let God judge him.

However, if you are a Christian you will pray for him, and you will never cease to pray until God works or until the end comes. God knows how to convict the sinner of his sinful ways. God can send catastrophe on him—yes, and on her too. God has more ways than one of answering prayer. "Have faith in God."

When your husband is fifty he will need you more than ever. When he is sixty he will need you still more. But when he is seventy you will be indispensable. Don't let love die then. Don't grow cold after the children are gone. Warm up to him more than ever. Do all you can to meet his needs. Don't take old age for granted and use it as an excuse for losing your interest and becoming indifferent.

Read Your Love-letters

Sometime, when you are going away alone, take your love-letters with you and read them over again. They will rekindle the flame of love. Then sit down and write some new ones. You should read your love-letters every five years. Don't wait until forty years have passed before you get them out. They will draw you together once again. You will see where you have failed and why. Then, when you have confessed it, God will knit your hearts together once more. Love is the great healer.

Don't stop writing love-letters after you are married. They should get better all the time. Perhaps after the children are gone you will write the best you ever wrote. You will need them then as never before, for you will need each other. So keep writing them, for, remember, love is the great healer.

It pays to leave each other for a week or two occasionally. You will find out how indispensable you are to each other then. While you are absent you can express your affection in letters and thus bring back the days of the past. Then, of course, the reunion will always be glorious. But don't stay away too long. Long separations are dangerous. True, absence makes the heart grow fonder, but there is always the temptation to find satisfaction and friendship in another if the separation is too long. Always be lovers and let the grace of God keep you true, so that you will have no regrets. You should express your love after you are married just the same as before.

There are two kinds of wives. There are those who love to demonstrate their affection. They meet you at the door, throw their arms around you and give you a welcoming kiss. They go to you of their own accord and crawl into your arms. If there is anything between they make it up at once. They are like a clinging vine and they are priceless. They know just how to make you love them and to make you happy.

Then there is the other kind. They are reserved. You have to take the initiative. They may love you more deeply than the first and they will express their affection for you in their letters. But they do not show it when they are with you. If there are any misunderstandings they just suffer and wait until *you* make up. Their love is true but undemonstrative. You will have to go more than halfway if you want to be happy. They have much to give, but they do not know how to give it, and you must teach them. You must win them. You must go the second mile. They may even resist you. Their response may be disappointing. But it will pay you to persevere.

What Saith the Lord?

Read carefully Paul's admonition in I Corinthians 7: 1–5, using Phillips' translation.

"Now let me deal with the questions raised in your letter. It is a good principle for a man to have no physical contact with woman. Nevertheless, because casual liaisons are so prevalent, let every man have his own wife and every woman her own husband. The husband should give his wife what is due to her as his wife, and the wife should be as fair to her husband. The wife has no longer full rights over her own person, but shares them with her husband. In the same way the husband shares his personal rights with his wife. Do not cheat each other of normal sexual intercourse unless, of course, you both decide to abstain temporarily, to make special opportunity for fasting and prayer. But afterwards you should resume relations as before, or you will expose yourselves to the obvious temptation of the devil."

Does it mean anything to you? Do you realize that it may be the solution to your problem? Your body, God says, is not your own. You thought it was. You withheld it when you should have given it. Husband and wife are one. That body of yours belongs to your husband and his to you, so both have privileges that neither has any right to deny. Have you learned to yield? If there is love you will.

You say you are too busy, too weary, and too old. Too busy for love? Too weary to express your affection? Too old to yield yourself to the one who loves to hold you in his arms and enjoy your response? Too cold to appreciate the touch of a lover's hand and to express a little of the affection in your heart?

Are you to live like two men or two women, or are you to live like man and wife? If you are in love, you will want to be with each other day and night. You will live your lives together. No longer will you be two; you will be one. Perhaps the reason for much of your unhappiness in married life now that the children are gone is found in 1 Corinthians 7: 1–5. You have drifted apart. You have not maintained the marriage relationship.

Woman Indispensable

Do you realize that woman was made for man and that he cannot get along without her? Listen! "Man was not created originally for the sake of woman, but woman was created for the sake of man" (1 Cor. 11: 9. Phillips). There are a few "career" women, so called, who can get along without a man, but there is no man who can get along and be his best without a woman. It is the woman who inspires, encourages, comforts and satisfies. It is because of the woman he can accomplish great things. His wife, therefore, holds the key to his happiness. She can break or make him. "It is not good that the man should be alone; I will make him an helpmeet for him" (Gen. 2: 18).

When you married him you said that you would take him "for better or for worse". See that you do it. Accept him for what he is. Don't expect to change him. Let God do that. If he does a lot of things you don't like and fails to do a lot of things you would like him to do, don't complain. Don't criticise. Don't find fault. Don't keep nagging him about them. It will only irritate him and drive him from you. Thank God that he loves you, that he has provided a home for you, that he thinks enough of you to want you with him, and that he is true to you. Forget the other things. Don't even expect them. Be content with what you have. Go to him with open arms. Take time to express your love. Give him an opportunity to enjoy your affection. Go to him often. Put your arms around him. Make love to him, even if he is old. Be so indispensable that he will never even think of anyone else.

Mary and Martha

You will glory in your home, in the way you keep it. You will pride yourself on your lovely table and your clothes. You will do your best to make your children attractive. Everything will be clean and orderly. Then you will expect him to see it and appreciate it and to say something about it. You will want him to compliment you, and you will be bitterly disappointed when he doesn't.

Well, if you are going to be a Martha and never a Mary, then that is what will happen. But if you will take time to sit down in communion and fellowship with him, as Mary did, you will get your reward. Nothing that Martha can do, important though it may be, can ever take the place of Mary's part. Men are won by Marys, not by Marthas. All the Marthas in the world could never win a man's heart. It is Mary who wins. Men would take Mary without Martha rather than Martha without Mary, if they could not have both. Martha cannot satisfy; Mary can. That is something many a woman needs to learn. It was Mary who pleased Jesus the most.

She Holds the Key

But why say so much about the wife, you ask? Is she not the weaker vessel? Yes and no. The wife holds the key. She is the rudder that guides the ship. Great men have great mothers. It is the woman's influence that counts most. What the wife is the husband will be. So has the Lord ordained. If the mother smokes and drinks the child is doomed. Not so the father. It is the woman's influence that tells. What a responsibility!

Last of all, don't argue. Quarrelling raises the blood-pressure. Submit. "No attack, no defence." Let that be your motto. Live peaceably (Rom. 12: 18). Nothing separates like argument. Give in, even if you know you are right. Don't be stubborn or dogmatic. Learn to yield. Better to remain silent than to antagonize. Argument creates feeling, and feeling temper. It may not be easy, but it is possible. Practise restraint. Take it to the Lord in prayer. If you feel that you are never wrong and if you can never apologize and say "I'm sorry", if you are always ready to argue the point, you will be certain to grieve the Holy Spirit and you will never be perfectly united in love. There will be an ugly chasm between. Therefore, if you want to be happy, don't argue. God's grace is always sufficient. Never forget that the husband is the head; he is the head to carry out his wife's plans as queen of the home.

Old age can be happy. There is still much to enjoy after the children are gone. Married life can be a heaven on earth—that is if both will play the game—for this is one game that no one can play alone. It takes two to win it, and it can only be won when it is played together; for it is the game of life, and once lost it is lost for ever. There is no second chance.

This, then, is my message for husbands and wives. There is much more that I could say, but I have said enough. May God solve the problems as you pray and live together. And may the twilight years of your life be the best. Then, after the children are gone, you will be all in all to each other.

CHAPTER XII

OUR GREATEST FOE

OUR greatest foe is "strong drink". You may catalogue all the perils of our country, pile them up one upon another until they are collected in one fearful, hideous mass, and the evils of strong drink will far outweigh them all. If you don't believe it, listen then to this saloon-keeper's advertisement:

"Friends and neighbours, I am grateful for past favours, and having supplied my store with a fine line of choice wines and liquors, allow me to inform you that I shall continue to make drunkards, paupers, and beggars for the sober, industrious, respectable members of the community to support.

"My liquors will excite riot, robbery and bloodshed. They will diminish your comforts, increase your expenses, and shorten your life. I can confidently recommend them as sure to multiply fatal accidents and incurable diseases.

"They will deprive some of life, others of reason, and all of peace. They will make fathers fiends, wives widows, children orphans, and all poor. I will train your sons in infidelity, dissipation, ignorance, lawlessness, and every other vice. I will thus accommodate the public; it may be at the loss of my never-dying soul, but I have a family to support—the business pays, and the public encourages it.

"I have paid my licence and the traffic is lawful, and if I don't sell it somebody else will. I know the Bible says 'Thou shalt not kill', and 'No drunkard shall enter the Kingdom of Heaven', but I want an easy living and I have resolved to gather the wages of iniquity and fatten on the ruin of my species.

"Should you doubt my ability, I refer you to the pawn-shops, the poor-house, the police court, the hospital, the penitentiary, and the gallows, where you will find many of my best customers have gone. A sight of them will convince you that I do what I say."

Greatest Criminal in History

Alcohol is a self-confessed criminal. In fact it is the world's greatest criminal. Listen to its confession:

"I am the greatest criminal in history. I have killed more men than have fallen in all the wars of the world. I have turned men into brutes. I have made millions of homes unhappy. I have transformed many ambitious youths into hopeless parasites. I make smooth the downward path for countless millions. I destroy the weak, and weaken the strong. I make the wise man a fool and trample the fool into his folly. I ensnare the innocent. The abandoned wife knows me; the hungry children know me; the parents whose child has bowed their grey heads in sorrow know me. I have ruined millions and shall try to ruin millions more."

Booze, the Mother of Crime

Judge Wm. M. Gemmill has this to say about it:

"Booze is the mother of crime. It gives life and sustenance to slums, dives, brothels, gambling dens, and 'pay-off joints'. It nerves to his deed the homicide, the stick-up man, the burglar, the thief, and the thug. It fires the brain of the prostitute and the panderer. It feeds and inflames the passions of the weak-minded and the degenerate.

"I have tried an army of 50,000 human derelicts, most of whom were booze-soaked. With faces red and bloated, with eyes dull and languid, with bodies weak and wasted, with clothing foul and ragged, this vast army is forever marching with unsteady step to the graves of the drunkard and the pauper or to the prison and workhouse.

"I have looked into the tear-stained faces of a still larger army of fathers and mothers, brothers and sisters, wives and husbands, as they have pleaded for the miserable wrecks that booze has made. I have seen with this army ten thousand pale-faced, hollow-cheeked, ragged, hungry, and starving children, cursed by booze.

"I have observed that every bandit crew that goes forth to murder starts from a saloon; that every panderer has his rendezvous in a grogshop; that every den of thieves makes its victims drunk before it robs them; that every house of prostitution has its bar or is in partnership with booze; that every gambling den either is in a saloon or sustains a close relationship with one; that the pick-pocket 'trust' is housed in a saloon; that the 'pay-off' joint for the crook and the crooked policeman is in a saloon; that the professional bondsmen and character witnesses for thieves and hold-up men are saloon-keepers or bartenders.

"Booze has caused 200,000 divorces in the United States in the last twenty years and adds 25,000 more to this number every year. It divides more homes, fills more jails, and empties more churches than all other influences combined.

"Judges, legislators, mayors, governors, and even presidents, sit dumb or quail in the presence of this monster, which enters millions of homes and leaves them desolate.

"I have witnessed daily its ravages after it had spent its wild fury upon the helpless bodies of women and children, or after it had reaped for a night, in the public dance, its harvest of virtue, now dead for ever. I have observed that the last man to be employed and the first to be discharged is a victim of booze.

"War may be hell; but where it slays its thousands, booze destroys its tens of thousands."

The Bar

In every saloon there is a bar. Here is something that was written by a life convict in Joliet Prison:

A Bar to heaven, a door to hell,
  Whoever named it, named it well;
A Bar to manliness and wealth,
  A door to want and broken health.

A Bar to honour, pride and fame,
  A door to grief and sin and shame;
A Bar to hope, a bar to prayer,
  A door to darkness and despair.

OUR GREATEST FOE

A Bar to honoured, useful life,
  A door to brawling, senseless strife;
A Bar to all that's true and brave,
  A door to every drunkard's grave.

A Bar to joys that home imparts,
  A door to tears and aching hearts;
A Bar to heaven, a door to hell,
  Whoever named it, named it well.

Three Classes

We have three classes of people to deal with. There are, first of all, those who have never experienced its horrors, who have never seen its hellish work. Hence, they do not realize what it is nor what it is doing and, as a result, they are uninterested. But let them learn by bitter experience just what it means to sit up until one or two in the morning watching for a drunken husband to come reeling home; let them see their little children starving, freezing and dying for want of the money spent on liquor; and let it go on night after night and day after day with no hope for a better, happier future— then they will understand.

The second class consists of what we designate "moderate drinkers". Many of them know the curse of liquor, but they happen to have wills strong enough to take it in moderate quantities and they like it too well to lift up their voices against it. They forget the heart-rending cry of Cain: "Am I my brother's keeper?" They claim that they are only responsible for themselves and not for those around them. The determination of Paul—"If meat make my brother to stumble I will eat no meat while the world lasts lest I make my brother to stumble"—has no place in their lives.

Oh, moderate drinker, do you know that you are the greatest stumbling-block, the most dangerous example of all? Do you know that young men by hundreds are going to imitate your actions, young men who have not the will-power of which you boast? Do you realize that they are going straight to a drunkard's grave, and that you are sending them there? Tell me, oh tell me, what are you going to say when those young men face you at the judgment bar of God?

When the Master asks them why they died as drunkards, you will see the finger of every last one of them pointed directly at you, and they will accuse you of their downfall. The crime will lie at your door, for they will be your victims. And then—for you will have no word to utter—amid the silence of the terrible verdict, will come the awful words: "No drunkard shall enter the Kingdom of Heaven. Depart from me into everlasting fire prepared for the devil and his angels." And all because you thought you had liberty to do as you liked! Oh, listen! "Take heed lest this liberty of yours becomes a stumbling-block to them that are weak, and through thy knowledge the weak brother perish, for whom Christ died."

Then there is the third class, those who sell, namely the liquor people. Some of them, a few, see no harm in it, and they are sincere in their opposition, though how it is possible it is hard to understand. But the majority of them know full well that they are in an illegitimate business, yet they fight as long as hope remains for the sake

of the money they make. For money, not the welfare of
their fellow men, is their great concern.

They claim that we are taking away what they call
"personal liberty", and they forget that it is the man who
has become the slave of drink who has been robbed of
every vestige of personal liberty. The habit has been
formed and he is powerless to break it. Drink he must—
yes, and drink he will, if it takes the coat off his back to
pay for it. Freedom has gone for ever, and he is a slave,
the slave of his appetite. It is only when a man has been
freed from the habit that personal liberty is restored.

But, after all, is personal liberty best? Listen! Personal
liberty says to the train: "You may jump the track and go
where you like." Intelligent liberty says: "No, you must
keep to the rails, and only within their bounds are you
free." Tell me, which is better? Personal liberty says:
"You have a right to whatever you see. Steal, it is yours."
And civil liberty answers: "No, you must recognize the
ownership of others." Personal liberty says: "Get drunk,
club your wife, beat your children, starve your family,
and murder your fellow men." But civil liberty responds:
"Do it at your peril, and, if you do, we will hang you."
Do we want personal liberty, then? God knows we don't.

Another argument is that prohibition throws men out
of work, takes bread from the mouths of dependent
children, and so is cruel and heartless—referring, of
course, to the children of the saloon-keeper. But they forget that prohibition is not enforced in a day; that ample
time is given to secure other work. And, worse still, they
forget about the thousands and tens of thousands that they
have ruined through their awful business; the starving of

millions of little children through the drink sold to their crazed fathers, and the money taken for liquor that should have gone for bread. Ah, they never think of that.

Weeping wives, crying children, broken-hearted mothers, separated families, starving millions, and hell-cursed homes—these necessarily follow and must be endured. So long as they get the money it does not matter; it is money. Let it be bought by blood, soaked in tears, and wrenched from hungry children—no matter, it is money. Blood money? Yes—but what of that? Silence conscience, take it, it was legally (?) earned. But let a few of the liquor men be thrown out of work to share the lot of the unemployed and it is barbarous.

Liquor is Always Evil

I think if your child got hold of poison you would be justified in taking it away. If there were rattlesnakes in the bed you would remove them before you put the child in. And the same holds true in regard to liquor. Here is a demon, a snake, a poison, and one of the worst kind. Some do not realize its danger, but let us remove it just the same. It is our duty to protect them.

But we are not fighting men. We have nothing against any individual as a man. What we are fighting is his abominable business. Let him get into honourable work and we will esteem him as highly as any man. If the liquor business were the last business on earth, I would joyfully yield up my life and die rather than take a cent from it. I would feel that every mouthful I ate had been purchased with blood money.

Women have told me that the great sorrow in their married life has been drink. Had it never entered their home they would have been supremely happy. It blights whatever it touches. It robs man of every principle of manhood and degrades him lower than the brute beast. Few can withstand its power. Once it takes hold it seldom lets go. Physical strength is lessened and brain power weakened. Men who might have held high positions must remain at the same level all their lives because of its hold upon them. Others have risen around them but they are left. Why, they do not know.

Drink, and drink alone, is the explanation in thousands of cases. Most of them go down so far that when they are past middle life they haven't as good a position as they had when they started. Drink has spoiled their every chance. Moral standards are polluted and degraded. Life that God intended should be noble and beautiful is debased, broken and wrecked. Ruin is written everywhere.

Do you know that it is the first glass that makes a man an alcoholic? You cannot tell me of anyone in the world who has ever become an alcoholic who has not taken the first glass. It is the first drink that is fatal. If a man never takes the first glass he will never become an alcoholic. Therefore it is the first drink that is most dangerous. I warn you not to take it. If you want to be certain that you will never become an alcoholic, then do not take your first drink. Of course, God does not speak of alcoholics. God speaks of drunkards. That is what an alcoholic is. He is a drunkard. Alcoholism is not a disease, it is a sin. If, therefore, you do not want to become a drunkard, do not take your first drink.

Alexander the Great rose to be a world conqueror, but Alexander the Great died a drunkard. It was drink that laid him low, and his four generals received the kingdom he had won. Robert Burns today holds the place of favourite poet in every Scottish heart, but Robert Burns will carry with him as long as time endures the scar of a blighted manhood, and that scar is the scar of drink.

The liquor traffic is a business that must be carried on behind stained windows, a business that cannot face the light of day. Things happen that must happen in the dark. Other businesses may be open and above board, but not so this. It is in league with the underworld; one of the most powerful agencies the devil has, and he always carries on his work in the dark.

Do you know that liquor is no longer listed as a medicine. It is classed as "a dangerous drug in the same category as opium for which a habit may be formed". And I got that on the authority of a reliable physician.

In the days of the old saloon women were barred. Seldom was a drunken woman seen on the streets. Only the lowest of the low ever indulged. But today all is changed. They have dressed up the saloons and called them beer parlours. And now the wives and daughters of husbands and fathers enter unashamed. At first they stepped down to the degrading habit of smoking cigarettes. Now they drink. God help us! Where will it end?

In the old days men could only hurt themselves; there were no cars. Today we are confronted with drunken drivers. And accidents in which lives are lost are of frequent occurrence.

Wrong to Licence the Liquor Traffic

We talk about "licence". Licence, my friends, may make a business legitimate according to law, but it doesn't alter it in the sight of God. Talk about a Christian nation —it doesn't exist. For as long as governments will consent to accept the proceeds of sin, and such a sin as the liquor traffic, the principles of Jesus Christ must be utterly ignored. "Legalized vice," "restricted evil"—God Almighty help us to get rid of such contradictory terms! The idea of a so-called Christian government sanctioning traffic in sin!

We are told that prohibition cannot be enforced. Well, the law against murder and theft has not been enforced in some countries. Does that mean that we are to do away with the law? Are we to let men murder whenever they want to, and steal without fear of punishment, simply because we can't enforce the law? I should say not! It is the duty of the government to see that the law is enforced; and if it cannot, then we had better ask it to resign and put one in that can.

There are those who tell us that conditions were worse during the days of Prohibition than they are now. And then they bring up the bootlegger and his nefarious traffic. Well, I lived during the Prohibition era and I want to stamp that statement as a downright lie.

In ten years of prohibition in Ontario (1917–1926) the convictions for violations of the Liquor Act other than for drunkenness—that is, mainly for bootlegging—averaged 4,230 per annum. In ten years ending 1939 the average convictions for violations of the Liquor Act other than for drunkenness totalled 5,566—an average increase per annum over Prohibition years of 1,336 or 32 per cent. This proves that the opening of the beverage-room does not lessen bootlegging, indeed it frequently provides a screen behind which the bootlegger hides.

Suppose there are bootleggers—what of it? Better a thousand times to have bootleggers than what we have today. What is a bootlegger? Just another criminal. Then let us deal with him as a criminal, and thus take our stand against the liquor traffic.

Seldom did I see a drunk on the streets during Prohibition days and hardly ever a drunken woman. Today they are myriad, including girls in their teens. In the days of Prohibition very few young people ever got the taste of strong drink. They could not get it openly. It was by no means easy to find. They were not tempted by it on every corner as they are now. Drinking has increased to a most alarming degree since Prohibition days.

"It is now twenty years since the repeal of prohibition in the United States," writes *The National Voice*. "We were promised less drinking, less bootlegging, and less crime. The records are now in. Has there been less drinking? There are now 484,804 legal liquor outlets, one for every 81 families. We have 4,000,000 alcoholics. F.B.I. reports that arrests for drunkenness during these twenty years have increased 197 per cent. Is there less crime? Congressional investigations make it clear that crime groups threaten to control our chief cities. Is there less bootlegging? The Commission says that there was never a year under Prohibition when as many bootleggers were arrested as in each and every year since."

OUR GREATEST FOE

Do you know why France fell? Marshal Pétain can tell you. He says: "Our soldiers were drunk and could not fight."

Do you know what the brewers say? Listen! "We want to get the beer-drinking habit instilled into millions of young men who do not at present know the taste of beer." What do you think of that?

Why was Prohibition enforced in Oahu for seventy-seven days after Pearl Harbour? Are the reports true that both soldiers and officers were drunk when Japan struck?

Why are liquor stores closed during strikes? What does it do to men that makes it so dangerous?

Today it is being served on ships, trains and planes. A lovely young hostess has to become a barmaid. All the joy has been taken out of travel by air because of the cigarette-, liquor-infested atmosphere. Passengers who want to be respectable are pressed to drink. What an insult! Some day it may be the cause of many an airplane crash.

Every Voter Guilty

Let me take you to a police court. Listen with me to the heart-rending words of a murderer. Picture the scene. Hear the judge as he puts his final question:

"Prisoner at the bar, have you anything to say why sentence of death shall not be passed upon you?"

A solemn hush fell over the crowded courtroom, and every person waited in almost breathless expectation for the answer to the judge's question.

The judge waited in dignified silence.

Not a whisper was heard anywhere, and the situation

had become painfully oppressive, when the prisoner was seen to move, his head was raised, his hand was clenched, and the blood had rushed into his pale, care-worn face.

Suddenly he arose to his feet and in a low, firm, but distinct voice said:

"I have! Your honour, you have asked me a question, and now I ask, as the last favour on earth, that you will not interrupt my answer until I am through.

"I stand here before this bar, convicted of the wilful murder of my wife. Truthful witnesses have testified to the fact that I was a loafer, a drunkard, and a wretch; that I returned from one of my long debauches and fired the fatal shot that killed the wife I had sworn to love, cherish and protect. While I have no remembrance of committing the fearful deed, I have no right to complain or to condemn the twelve good men who have acted as jury in the case, for their verdict is in accordance with the evidence.

"But may it please the court, I wish to show that *I am not alone responsible for the murder of my wife!*"

This startling statement created a tremendous sensation. The judge leaned over the desk, the lawyers wheeled around and faced the prisoner, the jurors looked at each other in amazement, while the spectators could hardly suppress their intense excitement. The prisoner paused a few seconds, and then continued in the same firm, distinct voice:

"I repeat, your honour, that I am not the only one guilty of the murder of my wife. The judge on this bench, the jury in the box, the lawyers within this bar, and most of the witnesses, including the pastor of the old church, are also guilty before Almighty God, and will have to stand with me before His judgment throne, where we shall be righteously judged.

"If it had not been for the saloons of my town I never would have become a drunkard; my wife would not have been murdered; I would not be here today, ready to be hurled into eternity. Had it not been for these human traps, I would have been a sober man, an industrious workman, a tender father and a loving husband. But to-day my home is destroyed, my wife murdered, my little children—God bless and care for them—cast out on the mercy of the world, while I am to be hanged by the strong arm of the State."

True, only too true! It is the government that is responsible. It is those who vote it in who are guilty. What right, I ask, has the State to condemn a drunken driver who runs down and kills a pedestrian when the State itself permits the sale of liquor and even allows advertising urging him to drink? Who is to blame? Is the criminal who murders when he is drunk the guilty one or the government that licences the beer parlour where he gets his liquor? Are we to deal with the effect or the cause? What a travesty of justice!

Government Insanity

Now comes the news that the government is going to build hospitals for alcoholics. Can you beat it? The lunatics are not all in the asylum yet. To test the sanity of a man we turn on the tap and tell him to dip out the water. If he does not know enough to turn off the tap he is insane. The government turns on the tap and lets the liquor flow, then spends the profits on hospitals to cure the drunkard. What folly! All that they make in taxes they spend on jails, asylums and hospitals. What a confession of guilt!

They would rather build a hospital at the bottom of the gully than erect a fence at the top. They do not believe that prevention is better than cure. Why build hospitals for alcoholics when alcoholics need not exist? Before long we may even have breweries themselves donating large sums of money for the maintenance of hospitals to cure the drunkards they themselves make. What a scandal!

There is nothing, absolutely nothing, that tries the missionary more than the sale of liquor to the natives. Duncan and Crosby had to meet it among the Indians of British Columbia. It turned quiet, harmless Indians into fiends of hell, and often resulted in murder. The missionaries of the South Sea Islands faced and fought it constantly. It was the one great barrier among the cannibals of the Pacific. And all around the coast of Africa it has worked its terrible ravages. The same ship that carried the Bible to the native savage also brought him the rum that made efforts at reclamation almost useless.

Condemned by the Bible

The Bible condemns strong drink. About that there can be no argument. Let me quote what it says.

"Do not drink wine nor strong drink . . . lest ye die" (Lev. 10: 9).

"Wine is a mocker, strong drink is raging; and whosoever is deceived thereby is not wise" (Prov. 20: 1).

"The drunkard . . . shall come to poverty" (Prov. 23: 21).

"Who hath woe? Who hath sorrow? Who hath contentions? Who hath babblings? Who hath wounds without cause? Who hath redness of eyes? They that tarry long at the wine; they that go to seek mixed wine. Look not thou upon the wine when it is red, when it giveth its colour in the cup, when it moveth itself aright. At the last it biteth like a serpent, and stingeth like an adder" (Prov. 23: 29–35).

"Woe unto them that rise up early in the morning, that they may follow strong drink; that continue until night, till wine inflame them! Woe unto them that are mighty to drink wine, and men of strength, to mingle strong drink" (Isa. 5: 11, 22).

"Woe unto him that giveth his neighbour drink, that puttest thy bottle to him, and makest him drunken" (Hab. 2: 15).

"Drink neither wine nor strong drink" (Luke 1: 15).

"Be not deceived, neither . . . drunkards . . . shall inherit the Kingdom of God" (1 Cor. 6: 10).

Only One Cure

There is only one sure cure, the Lord Jesus Christ. He, and He alone, can make the drunkard sober. No one else can take away the desire for drink. Drunkards in thousands have been delivered. I would rather invest a dollar in the preaching of the Gospel of Jesus Christ to the slaves of drink than $10,000,000 towards a hospital for their cure. I have a Saviour who can break every fetter and set the prisoner free.

There is only one remedy for the liquor traffic. We must

stop it at the source. The manufacture of strong drink will have to be prohibited. There is no other cure. We must outlaw the brewery. It must be made a major crime to distil liquor. If it is not made it will not be sold. If there is no liquor there will be no drinking. Strong drink, like slavery, as a deadly evil, must be abolished.

There was a time when there was little or no sentiment against slavery. But finally the conscience of man was awakened. It took years, but it came. People laughed and ridiculed. Slavery had existed for centuries, they argued. What power could stop it? At last the Civil War broke out and slavery passed away. Where will you find a man who will uphold it today? Who would dare say that slavery was right, slavery is Christian? Its advocates have long since disappeared.

Some day, please God, every government in the world will abolish it. Like leprosy and poison, it will be outlawed, for it will be recognized as the most deadly evil ever fostered on the human race. Some day our children will wonder why we had to struggle so hard, why we did not prohibit it long ago, and the liquor traffic will have none to take its side. The Millennium is coming. Christ will yet reign. God speed the day! It cannot come too soon.

IMPORTANT!

Be a "Missionary" to some of your best Christian friends. If this book has stirred your soul, if the Cry of the World rings in your ears, if you sincerely want to do something to inspire others to put FIRST THINGS FIRST, lend this book to a Pastor or a Christian friend. Better still, buy one or more copies, distribute them and you will be giving something, the value of which cannot be compared to its nominal cost.

Copies of this book can be obtained by writing to any of the addresses in the front of the book.